Artificial Intelligence in BASIC

Mike James

Newnes Technical Books

Newnes Technical Books
is an imprint of the Butterworth Group
which has principal offices in
London, Boston, Durban, Singapore, Sydney, Toronto, Wellington

First published 1984

© **Butterworth & Co (Publishers) Ltd, 1984**
Borough Green, Sevenoaks, Kent TN15 8PH, England

All rights reserved. No part of this publication may be reproduced or transmitted in any form or by any means, including photocopying and recording, without the written permission of the copyright holder, application for which should be addressed to the Publishers. Such written application must also be obtained before any part of this publication is stored in a retrieval system of any nature.

This book is sold subject to the Standard Conditions of Sale of Net Books and may not be re-sold in the UK below the net price given by the Publishers in their current price list.

British Library Cataloguing in Publication Data

James, Mike
 Artificial Intelligence in BASIC.
 1. Artificial intelligence—Data processing
 2. Microcomputers—Programming   3. BASIC
 (Computer program language)
 I. Title
 001.53′5′0285424   QA335

 ISBN 0-408-01373-7

Library of Congress Cataloging in Publication Data

James, Mike.
 Artificial Intelligence in BASIC.

 Bibliography: p.
 Includes index.
 1. Artificial intelligence—Data processing.
 2. BASIC (Computer program language)   I. Title.
 Q336.J36   1984   001.53′5   84-3184
  ISBN 0-408-01373-7

Photoset by Butterworths Litho Preparation Department
Printed in England by Page Bros Ltd, Norwich, Norfolk

Preface

Artificial intelligence (AI) is a very interesting subject. However, there is a tendency to talk about AI rather than to do AI since the problems that AI tries to solve are generally very difficult. Also AI programs are usually too long to present as part of the discussion. The effect is that methods are described, results are catalogued but actual AI software is rarely seen.

This book presents some of the central ideas of AI complete with programs to illustrate the methods. All that is required is a knowledge of BASIC programming and a personal computer running BASIC.

As well as trying to present a coherent view of many separate parts of AI, the main purpose of this book is to show that practical applications of AI are now possible. By trying out the program examples and discovering what they can do for just a little programming effort, the enthusiastic programmer should gain sufficient confidence in the methods to commit time to developing real products.

This book began as a series of articles in *Electronics and Computing Monthly* and I would like to thank its publisher, Dave Raven, for his encouragement. I would also like to thank Steve Oakey for widening my interest in AI and to Vartkes Goetcherian for engaging in many long discussions concerning expert systems.

This book is dedicated to my son Samuel Michael – my own project in natural intelligence.

M.J.

Contents

1	Computer intelligence: fact, fiction and future	1
2	The heuristic approach	9
3	When heuristics meet: the strategy of competition	28
4	Thinking and reasoning: expert systems	40
5	The structure of memory	65
6	Pattern recognition	82
7	Language	100
8	Approaching intelligence	113
	Further reading	123
	Index	125

1

Computer Intelligence: Fact, Fiction and Future

A recurring theme in science ficition is the development or construction of a computer that rivals man's intelligence. Although this is science fiction at the moment, it may not be the case for very much longer. Research labs all over the world are trying to produce computers that have some human characteristics: speaking computers, seeing computers, thinking computers. Whether or not these researchers ever reach their ultimate goal of equalling, or even exceeding human mental capacities, is in somes senses less important for us than the progress that they are making in each separate area. For, although it is certain that a truly intelligent computer would require some very sophisticated hardware to hold all of its programming, some of the smaller, but very exciting, aspects of intelligence can already be duplicated on home computers!

Most of the research that goes on in Artificial Intelligence, or AI as it is usually called, is a little difficult to understand. Not because it is difficult but because it is the result of many years of research by academics and engineers who are really only concerned with communicating with other academics and engineers who already know a lot about the subject. This leaves the interested beginner out in the cold! The purpose of this book is to explain those ideas of AI that can be used to produce programs on today's microcomputers and thus to provide as practical an introduction to AI as possible. The practical component of this book takes the form of programs written in BASIC. These programs serve both to illustrate the topics under discussion and to give readers a starting point for their research. While it is true that much of the most advanced AI work needs powerful and very expensive computers, it is very possible for low cost private research to find a way of doing something that has been overlooked. AI is about software development and as such is a subject that all programmers can take part in. It is important that you type in and use the example programs because there is a lot of excitement in using an AI program that is impossible to convey in writing and by using even the simple programs you will be able to assess how much intelligence it is possible to produce with very limited resources.

Know your computer's IQ

You may find the suggestion that your small home computer is capable of running programs that reproduce some aspect of human behaviour difficult to believe. After all, isn't it the case that your machine can't even cope with mundane programs fast enough? Isn't it true that it is always running out of memory in the middle of program development?

However, if you look at the range of programs that a typical home computer might be running it is possible to detect two different types. Some programs are straightforward but put heavy demands on the computer's speed of calculation. For example, 'arcade' games with moving graphics are, believe it or not, very simple from the point of view of logic but, if they are to work convincingly, they have to work *very* fast and this is where the difficulty in producing them comes from. Other programs are difficult to write because it is hard to follow what they are supposed to do and making them do it faster is a secondary problem! For example, a program to play chess is a challenge because the logic of chess playing is far from obvious. Once you have worked out the logic of the program it is likely that you will come up against the problems of shortage of memory or lack of speed but these problems are simple compared to the initial one. The fact that chess programs do exist for the smallest micro should make you stop and think about the real capabilities of your humble machine. Playing chess is a comparatively intelligent act and your micro can do it!

If we look at the evidence then we are forced to the conclusion that today's micros have higher potential intelligence than most of the simple software that they run would lead us to believe.

Commercial intelligence

The importance of AI programs has not gone entirely unnoticed by the commercial software producers and in the near future we should see the introduction of an increasing number of 'clever' programs. The capabilities of programs tend to evolve because of market forces. If you are the first to produce a particular piece of software then it can be very basic and still be very successful since people have no choice but to buy it. When other software companies launch similar products they must add extra options and improvements if they want people to buy their product in preference to the original. At some point, however, the product reaches a state of refinement that cannot easily be bettered and to make any sort of impression on the market a new software vendor has to think up something new. In this case new usually means an increase in the cleverness of the program.

A good example of this is in the field of word processing packages. The first word processing programs simply allowed text to be altered and formatted. Later programs contained improvements such as allowing footnotes and compiling book indexes. A major jump in this steady stream of improvements was the introduction of spelling and text checking programs. These carry out many of the tedious tasks of proof reading that once needed an intelligent human. Even now the intelligence of these programs is increasing. One proof-reading program now claims to check and offer advice on grammar. Where will it end!?

Apart from chess playing and proof reading, other areas of AI that are being exploited commercially include decision analysis (programs that can help a human operator to make a correct decision in difficult situations), expert systems (programs that can solve problems in specified areas) and program writing (programs such as THE LAST ONE and PEARL which generate programs from descriptions of a problem). However, it seems likely that there are many more exciting applications for AI that remain unexplored at the moment either because the theories lie hidden in academic journals or simply because the people who know about them are not interested in commercial applications. There is no doubt that AI will become increasingly important in every area of computer use.

Computer-Aided Intelligence

Before moving on to consider the different areas of AI that we will cover in later parts of this book, there is still something that we can learn from a consideration of the proof reading, spelling and grammar programs. There are many areas of human intelligence that it is *not* possible to copy using current (or in some cases forseeable) technology. This doesn't provide a good reason for not exploring the use of computers in these areas, however. Many people probably recognised the desirability of a program that could check spelling but rejected it because it effectively meant teaching a computer to spell and who wouldn't abandon such a project before it had even begun! The breakthrough came when someone realised that a spelling check program can be written quite easily if a human is available to resolve any questions of spelling that cannot be determined using a computer dictionary. So the spelling program checks each word against its internal dictionary and if it finds it carries on to the next word. If the word isn't present then the program pauses and asks the human operator if the spelling is correct. If it is then the word is added to the dictionary and the human is never bothered for the correct spelling of that word again. It could be said that the program 'learns' the correct spellings of new words.

Notice that the key to producing a spelling program is lowering your sights from the ambitious 'work alone' program to the simpler but almost as useful 'human assisted' program. It is often the case in AI that the complete solution to a problem is a topic for research but a partial 'human aided' solution is a lot easier and produces a very useful program that combines the accuracy of the computer and the flexibility of a human.

This idea of machine intelligence mixing with human intelligence is a new and almost unexplored notion. As time goes on we can expect to see computers acting increasingly in this way as 'intelligence amplifiers'. Traditional programs can be thought of as capturing or summarising a tiny part of the programmer's knowledge and intelligence and making it available to the user to carry out some specific job. In this sense, we have been using computers as very limited capacity intelligence stores. What has to be done in the future is to provide software that captures a more complex and general sort of intelligence that can be seen as an aid to the thinking of its human user.

What is intelligence?

The trouble with the term AI is that, although the meaning of the word 'artificial' is clear enough, it is difficult to be precise about the meaning of 'intelligence'. The traditional answer given by psychologists – "intelligence is what intelligence tests measure" – is totally useless in the area of computer intelligence. If we were to interpret the word intelligence in this way then AI research would be confined to discovering ways of answering the questions on intelligence tests. The result would be a computer that could answer 'trick' questions very well but couldn't see or speak or hear etc. The trouble is that intelligence tests assume that there is something called 'intelligence' present in the first place – they may measure intelligence but they do not *detect* its presence! Rather than continuing in this vein, provoking a flood of philosophical arguments, it is more sensible to summarise the areas that are normally considered to be part of the AI field of study to illustrate what can be included.

It is not easy to give a complete categorisation of the areas of AI because there is so much overlap and interaction but for the sake of simplicity we can identify the following areas:

computer vision; speech production; speech/voice recognition; thinking, reasoning and problem solving; language understanding and translation.

Underlying all of these areas is the fundamental distinction between a program that is written to solve a problem and a program that 'learns'. For example, it might be that you could write a program that could make measurements that would tell the difference between a circle and a square or it might be possible to write a program that could *learn* the difference. Some people feel that programs that learn are the essence of AI but I feel that this ignores far too many of the interesting fixed-strategy programs to be useful. To avoid any more discussion of what intelligence, or AI, is we will consider each of the areas in turn and consider what sort of things we can hope to achieve on a typical microcomputer.

Vision and recognition

Machine vision is a very important area of research because the increasing use of robots in industry depends on it. For a reasonable sum, it is possible to buy small robot arms that can be attached to most makes of micro. These arms can be used to move objects around with little difficulty as long as some way can be found to tell the machine where the objects are, because without vision the machine is restricted to blind movements. The trouble with computer vision is that, firstly, it needs some very expensive hardware – a TV camera at least – and, secondly, it does require a very fast computer. The information in a typical scene is so vast that even the fastest computers have trouble doing even the simplest analysis in a reasonable amount of time.

Computer vision is, sadly, one area of AI that is out of the reach of all but a small number of dedicated enthusiasts. This doesn't mean that we have to ignore the area altogether because there are many interesting and enjoyable spin offs from vision research that are accessible to any small computer with even a limited graphics option. We can examine the way that simple shapes can be recognised and even try a simple letter recognition program that could form the basis for a reading system if coupled to some extra hardware. These topics are covered in Chapter Six.

Speech production

The area of speech production or synthesis is perhaps one of the most commercially successful AI has come up with to date. You can buy computers which have special speech chips that can produce any word in a vocabulary of around 200 words. Because this particular AI solution has been realised in hardware, there is very little worthwhile that can be done with software on a standard micro. If your micro does not have speech synthesis then it is easier and cheaper to buy the necessary hardware than to try to write your own software. It is worth looking at the principles that lie behind speech generation but apart from this there is very little practical that can be done. However, if you already have a speech synthesiser, then much of the material included in Chapter Seven about language and language understanding will help you to get the best from it.

Speech and voice recognition

Like speech production, this topic is best handled by special purpose hardware. There are a number of add-on boards that will allow home computers to recognise one of a small number of words. Because of the extra hardware required, this book does not deal with speech recognition directly, but much of the material concerning recognition in general, and language in particular, will help you understand and make best use of any hardware that you might buy.

Language understanding and translation

The goal of language understanding is to produce a program that will carry on a sensible conversation with a user. Language translation may seem like a simpler task because all you have to do is to use a translation dictionary. In fact, good language translation requires a good deal of language understanding to avoid silly translations of idiomatic expressions such as 'keep your nose to the grindstone'.

Complete language understanding is not possible using a micro, as it would run out of memory far too quickly and there is also the small matter that no one really knows how to do it! However, by studying what is known about language, it is possible to produce some very useful programs. In particular, you can write a small program that will carry on a restricted conversation with you, and analyse written material to find out how difficult it is to read. Also, a study of the grammar of English can throw much light on the area of compuer languages.

Thinking, reasoning and problem solving

This is the largest area of AI and is really a catch-all for everything that doesn't obviously fit into one of the previous categories. Thinking, reasoning and problem solving are definitely things that humans do but they are in general associated very closely with other actions. For example, we very often receive problems via language or sight and this tends to confuse the act of problem solving. To study these problems, it is necessary to work in small, well-defined areas that provide problems that are easy to specify to a computer. One of the first areas of problem solving to be tackled was mathematical theorem proving. A program was written that would accept a statement in mathematics and provide a complete proof. Many of the theorems proved would have taken a mathematics graduate some time to solve so the program was simulating a fairly advanced reasoning process but it could not produce any new results and, in this sense, it was a very dull sort of 'thinker'. Even though creativity is still beyond the reach of even the largest computer, thinking and reasoning have become growth areas of AI that even the smallest home micro can become involved in, as we discover in Chapter Four.

One of the best known areas of problem solving is game playing. A great deal of effort has gone into devising methods of getting computers to play a good 'human-like' game of chess. It is not really possible to pursue chess programs using BASIC because of their size and speed requirements. It may come as a surprise, however, that there are a number of simpler games that provide excellent illustrations of computer problem solving. Computer game playing is such a good introduction to ideas that are fundamental to AI that the next two chapters are devoted to this subject.

Included in thinking, reasoning and problem solving is the activity known as learning. There is in fact an entire subject devoted to machines that learn – cybernetics. More precisely, cybernetics is the study of machines that can adjust themselves to suit their surroundings. Here we meet concepts that are familiar to electronics engineers such as feedback and control loops. It is quite possible to write programs in BASIC that learn or adjust to their surroundings and in Chapter Eight we will examine this problem.

The subject of learning brings us to the area of memory. Human memory is very different from the standard Random Access Memory

(RAM) that is to be found inside every computer. Human memory is in one sense very disorganised: if you try to recall one thing the chances are that you will also recall a lot of things that are related to it. Human memory is said to be 'associative' because things are not just stored but are stored in relation to things that they are associated with. It is possible to write a simulation of the way memory works on a fairly small computer. We will look at how to do this in Chapter Five.

Computability

Computability is the name of a branch of mathematics that tries to discover what computers can and cannot do. By trying to find the theoretical limitations on computers we might manage one day to answer the fundamental question: is the human brain simply a very complicated computer or does it embody some principle that is yet to be discovered? If we are nothing more than computers (which is my own view) then the limits that are discovered for computers are also limits on us. Computability will be the only really non-practical subject considered in any detail in this book (see Chapter 8), but it is included because it offers a fascinating insight into how we reason about the world.

Back to BASIC

As already mentioned, the examples given in this book will be written in BASIC. BASIC isn't really the best language for writing AI programs, but it is the most popular language on micros and this fact makes it worth the inconvenience of using it. However using a language such as BASIC does at least prove that AI techniques are general programming methods and don't depend on any special facilities available in languages such as Lisp and PROLOG that are more often used in AI. The dialect of BASIC used is standard Microsoft BASIC and as no special graphics etc are used it should be easy to convert to any machine. In fact, on many machines no conversion as such will be necessary. You may, however, want to add graphics and sounds to make the programs more interesting. As many of the programs will be concerned with implementing advanced AI methods, advanced BASIC techniques will be introduced. So you should be able to pick up some useful ways of using BASIC by reading the programs.

2

The heuristic approach

To be able to write a program that solves a problem, it is necessary to know how *you* would go about solving it. Anyone who has even the slightest practical knowledge of computers knows that there is no way of getting one to answer a question simply by asking it; someone at some time must have 'programmed' the answer. The trouble is that there are many problems that humans do not know the solution to and naturally enough these are the very problems that we would like computers to solve. What is more surprising is that it is very often possible for a human to solve a problem without knowing *how* it was solved. But to be able to write a program to solve a problem, it is not only necessary to be able to solve the problem, it is also necessary to be able to describe how the solution is arrived at. The reason for this is that the program that you are trying to write *is* actually a description of how you solved the problem! One approach to AI claims that it doesn't matter if we don't know how to go about solving a specific problem, the important thing to do is to write programs that can solve problems in general, in the same way that humans do. Following this approach, you could end up with a program that is a general problem-solver and may solve specific problems but it too may not be able to 'tell you' how it did it! This idea sounds very promising but so far very little progress has been made. A simpler alternative is to press on with the attempt to write programs that solve specific problems even though the complete method of solution may not be known.

Solving problems

Consider the problem of winning at chess or draughts. There are some humans who solve this problem very well. They tend to win against most opponents and this suggests that they have a method of playing which is a good solution to the problem. If you couldn't find such experts then you might decide that there was no solution to the chess/draughts problem. In other words, you might assume that players made moves for a wide variety of reasons, none of which had anything much to do with the strategy of the game, and the winner was fairly random!

The existence of people who perform consistently better than beginners and the internal feelings of 'working things out' when you are playing such a game both suggest that humans do have a 'program' inside their heads for solving the problems they present. But if you try to explain how you play chess or draughts you are very likely to fail! You might be able to manage vague generalisations or very complicated justifications for particular moves but, if you try to write a program to play in your place, you will soon discover how poor your knowledge is.

For some games it is possible to give a few simple rules that if followed guarantee that you will win or at the very worst draw. For example, the game of noughts and crosses can be summed up in this way and once someone has worked out the rules, the game becomes very boring. (It is still an interesting challenge to try and write a program that uses the rules to always win or at least draw). Games such as chess or draughts, however, are so complex that as yet no one has managed to give any set of rules that guarantees a win. It may be that it is impossible to do this or it may be that someone will eventually work out what we have all been missing and reduces chess and draughts to the level or noughts and crosses!

So the current state of affairs is that there are many problems that humans solve that are very difficult, if not impossible, to reduce to the application of a set of rules that guarantee a solution.

Heuristics

Traditionally a program is a list of instructions for giving a sure solution to a problem or reporting that no solution exists. Such a list of instruction is called an *algorithm* and algorithms are the core of computer science and programming to date. However, as already pointed out, there are many problems that we have not found algorithmic solutions to and if computer science is to develop we must make progress in these areas. If you examine the way that you solve problems then you might notice that very often what you are doing is not using an algorithm but applying a loose collection of rules that 'seem' to work. For example, in chess you might hold to the rule 'control the middle of the board' and while this, and other rules like it, cannot guarantee you find a solution (i.e. a win) it makes it more likely that you will get closer to one. A rule that tends to get closer to a solution is known as a *heuristic* and while it might seem to you that a heuristic is a 'second class' algorithm, this is far from the truth! Heuristics may not be able to guarantee you a solution to a problem, and they cannot tell you when a solution doesn't exist, but they can be used in a wide range of situations. Furthermore, when they do come up with a solution, it can be in much less time than an algorithm would take for the same problem. Future computer science and programming is almost certainly going to be more about heuristic and combined heuristic–algorithmic approaches to problem solving.

Computer and human heuristics

Finding a heuristic still seems like a very difficult task and perhaps we are not very much better off. The sort of heuristics that humans use are often difficult to discover and difficult to express but this need not worry us too much. We are trying to find heuristics that are effective when carried out by a computer and computers work very fast. It is therefore easier to find simple heuristics and allow computers to apply them repeatedly or in very clever ways. In general, it's not so much the quality of the heuristic that matters; it's the way that the computer uses it. You could say that a simple heuristic applied a great many times is likely to be as good as a complex heuristic applied a few times. However, such generalisations are dangerous and as we will see it is sometimes important to be careful to utilise a heuristic fully.

In the rest of this Chapter, and the next, the idea of a heuristic will be explored by way of playing games. However, while games make excellent examples it is important to realise that heuristics are capable of tackling serious problems. Indeed, there are problem areas where, currently at least, algorithms are unable to provide any solutions and where heuristics provide the only possible approach. Such areas include the whole range of practical scheduling problems: timetabling and route planning and decisions like how to cut shapes out of cloth or other materials with minimum waste.

The tile game

The tile game is excellent material for trying out many ideas from artificial intelligence. In particular, it demonstrates most of the elements of implementing any game on a computer, it has a board of sorts, a set of rules that govern what constitutes a legal move and it is difficult to find an algorithm to solve it. Most people will already be familiar with the tile game in one variation or another. The most basic version of the game, and the one that we will use, is to take 8 tiles, numbered 1 to 8 and place them randomly into a square pattern leaving one empty space. For example.

3	4	2
1	5	
6	7	8

The object of the game is to move tiles into the empty space, keeping the overall square shape and to arrive at a final arrangement such as

1	2	3
4	5	6
7	8	

Before you read on, try the game yourself and investigate the way that you decide to make a move. As a youngster, I had a small moulded plastic version of this puzzle with the tiles slotted into one another so that you could slide them around the board but could not remove them or cheat! In case, like me, you no longer have such a toy handy, the following short program will enable you to play it via your micro. It is written in a fairly restricted version of Microsoft BASIC so you should have little trouble in getting it to run on your machine.

```
10  K=0
20  DIM B(3,3)
30  FOR I=1 TO 3
40  FOR J=1 TO 3
50  K=K+1
60  B(I,J)=K
70  NEXT J
80  NEXT I

90  I=3
100 J=3
110 FOR K=1 TO 20
120 X=INT(RND(0)*3)-1
130 Y=INT(RND(0)*3)-1
140 IF I+X>3 OR I+X<1 THEN GOTO 120
150 IF J+Y>3 OR J+Y<1 THEN GOTO 120
155 IF ABS(X)+ABS(Y)>1 OR X+Y=0 THEN GOTO 120
```

```
160 T=B(I,J)
170 B(I,J)=B(I+X,J+Y)
180 B(I+X,J+Y)=T
190 I=I+X
200 J=J+Y
210 NEXT K

220 M=1
230 K=0
240 S=0
250 FOR I=1 TO 3
260 FOR J=1 TO 3
270 K=K+1
280 IF B(I,J)<>K THEN S=1
290 IF B(I,J)=9 THEN PRINT "  ";:X=I:Y=J
300 IF B(I,J)<>9 THEN PRINT B(I,J);" ";
310 NEXT J
320 PRINT
330 NEXT I
340 IF S=0 THEN PRINT "SOLVED":STOP
350 PRINT "MOVE ";M
360 PRINT "MOVE WHICH TILE";
370 INPUT N
380 IF N<1 OR N>8 THEN GOTO 350
390 FOR I=1 TO 3
400 FOR J=1 TO 3
410 IF B(I,J)=N THEN A=I:B=J
420 NEXT J
430 NEXT I
440 IF ABS(X-A)+ABS(Y-B)>1 THEN GOTO 350
450 T=B(X,Y)
460 B(X,Y)=B(A,B)
470 B(A,B)=T
480 M=M+1
490 GOTO 230
```

A program to solve the tile problem

If you look at the listing of the automatic tile program below you should be able to see that it is made up of a number of subroutines. Each subroutine carries out a different part of playing the tile game and the program is really not a single program but a collection of subroutines that can be used in different ways to explore the problem. Each subroutine will be described in enough detail that it should be possible for you to replace it by a better, or just different, version.

The program is written in a fairly standard Microsoft BASIC and should present no conversion problems. Statements that might need changing before you run it on your micro are those concerning the string array M$. For example, ZX-BASIC requires line 30 to be replaced by

30 DIM M$(9, 4)

and line 6010 by

6010 J=VAL(M$(P,I))

The function RND(0) is assumed to produce random numbers in the range 0 to 1 and the function VAL(S$) will convert a number in the string S$ to numeric form.

```
10 REM AUTOMATIC TILE PROGRAM
20 DIM B(9)
30 DIM M$(9)
40 DIM M(9)
50 M=0
60 Q=0
70 GOSUB 3000
80 GOSUB 1000
90 GOSUB 2000
100 GOSUB 4000
110 GOSUB 5000
120 IF S=0 THEN GOTO 180
130 GOSUB 6000
140 GOSUB 7000
150 M=M+1
160 GOSUB 2000
170 GOTO 110
180 PRINT:PRINT
190 PRINT "SOLVED IN ";M
200 END

1000 FOR I=1 TO 9
1010 B(I)=I
1020 NEXT I
1030 P=9
1040 N=INT(RND(0)*10)+25
1050 FOR Z=1 TO N
1060 GOSUB 6000
1070 GOSUB 7000
1080 NEXT Z
1090 Q=0
1100 RETURN

2000 PRINT
2010 FOR I=1 TO 9
2020 PRINT B(I);" ";
2030 IF I=INT(I/3)*3 THEN PRINT
2040 NEXT I
2050 RETURN
```

The heuristic approach

```
3000 M$(1)="24  "
3010 M$(2)="135 "
3020 M$(3)="26  "
3030 M$(4)="157 "
3040 M$(5)="2468"
3050 M$(6)="359 "
3060 M$(7)="48  "
3070 M$(8)="579 "
3080 M$(9)="68  "
3090 M(1)=2
3100 M(2)=3
3110 M(3)=2
3120 M(4)=3
3130 M(5)=4
3140 M(6)=3
3150 M(7)=2
3160 M(8)=3
3170 M(9)=2
3180 RETURN

4000 FOR I=1 TO 9
4010 IF B(I)=9 THEN P=I
4020 NEXT I
4030 RETURN

5000 S=0
5010 FOR I=1 TO 9
5020 IF I<>B(I) THEN S=1
5030 NEXT I
5040 RETURN

6000 I=INT(RND(0)*M(P))+1
6010 J=VAL(MID$(M$(P),I,1))
6020 RETURN

7000 T=B(P)
7010 B(P)=B(J)
7020 B(J)=T
7030 Q=P
7040 P=J
7050 RETURN
```

Before you can start to write any game playing program, you have to decide on how to represent the 'board'. For the tile game, it is easier to ignore the fact that the board is two dimensional and use the array M with nine elements, one for each position that a tile can occupy. Each position is numbered so that, when the final arrangement is reached, tile one will be in M(1), tile two in M(2) and so on. The empty space can be represented by any convenient symbol but it makes life easier if it is a number, and 9 is the most obvious choice. To find out what tile is at position I, simply look at M(I).

Using the representation, it is easy to print the board out (subroutine 2000) and to check to see if the final winning position has been reached (subroutine 5000). It is not quite so easy to set up a starting position, however. The problem is to set up the tiles in a random order in such a way that they could have been produced by legal moves of the tiles. If you just generate a completely unconstrained random order for the tiles you can produce a starting arrangement that cannot be moved to the final arrangement without effectively lifting one of the tiles out of the frame! (The reason for this is that there are two versions of the tile game, a lefthanded version and a righthanded version and you cannot convert one to the other using nothing but legal moves!) The solution is to set the board up in its final or target position and then 'scramble' it by way of a random sequence of legal moves. Subroutine 1000 sets up a random board by shuffling a board previously set up in the final position. This has the additional advantage that the difficulty of the problem can be controlled by the degree of shuffling. The more the board is shuffled away from the final position, the harder it should be to solve.

The final problem is to detect illegal moves. The best and quickest way to do this is to set up a table that lists all the possible moves for any position of the 'space' (the 9 in this representation). If you look at subroutine 3000, you will see that the string array M$ is initialised to contain lists of legal moves. For example if the 'space' is at position 3 on the board then looking at M$(3) gives the string "26" which should be taken to mean that you can move the tile in position 2 or the tile in position 6 into the 'space' but no other moves are legal. This easy representation of legal moves for any position of the 'space' is the main reason that the tile game can be programmed efficiently in BASIC.

The only other subroutine that deserves mention at this stage is subroutine 7000, which will make any move specified by P, the current of the 'space', and J, the position of the tile to be moved into the 'space'. Obviously this is just a swap between M(P) and M(J) and the new position of the 'space' is J which can be placed into P to keep the current position updated.

Searching for a solution

Using just three subroutines, it is possible to write a crude tile game program. This crude program is contained in the program listed. First a move counter M is initialised and then subroutines

The heuristic approach

3000,1000,2000 and 4000 are called. This part of the program is always the same and simply sets up the move table (3000), initialises the board (1000) and then prints it out (2000). Subroutine 4000 has not been discussed before but its role is to locate the position of the 'space' into P after the board has been shuffled. This only has to be done once because the position of the 'space' is tracked by the move subroutine 7000 and is always in P. The attempt to find the solution begins with a check to discover if the solution has been found, by calling subroutine 5000. If it hasn't, i.e. S<>0, then the only thing to do is make a move. In this first simple program the move to be made is picked at random from the legal moves by subroutine 6000. In general terms, subroutine 6000 is acting as a 'move generator'. Picking a legal move at random is easy with the legal move table, M$. If there are three possible moves then all we have to do is generate a number between one and three and extract the corresponding character from the string M$(P). The number of legal moves for the position P is stored in M(P), line 6000 generates the random number between 1 and M(P) and line 6010 picks the correct character from M$(P). This random move is then carried out by calling subroutine 7000, the board is printed and then the whole cycle is repeated beginning with the check to see if the final position has been reached.

You might believe that such a simple problem as this could be solved by computer using random moves in a fairly short time. After all, the computer works so fast that it can afford to make any hundreds of wrong moves before finally making a right one. The truth is that even though a computer can quickly make many random moves it still takes a long time to find the answer. I have yet to see this simple method yield an answer even after running it for 24 hours and over one hundred thousand moves!

A heuristic for the tile game

If you watch the random movements produced by the previous program, you cannot help but despair as it fails to take even the most obvious move that would improve the situation. Even if by some quirk of fate it gets within one move of success it would be just as likely to take the wrong option and start to disorder the pattern again! The onlooker quickly comes to the conclusion that there must be a better approach to the problem, even though no algorithm exists for its solution.

If we were to have some measure of how far away from the final arrangement the current arrangement was then we could use a fairly obvious heuristic and select the move that takes the arrangement 'closer' to the desired arrangement.

The only problem is to decide what we mean by 'closer'. If you look at the current position of any tile then you can describe how far it is away from its final position by counting how many horizontal and vertical moves it would take to move it to its final position, ignoring the 'space'. For example, the 6 in the following arrangement could be moved to its final position by one move down and two moves across, and so it is three moves from 'home'.

6	3	1
2	4	8
	5	7

Notice that it doesn't matter that you couldn't move the 6 along this route because the 'space' is in the bottom left corner. We are only interested in using this as a rough measure of how far the 6 is from its final place. This measure of how far a tile is from its final place is known as the 'city block distance' because it is the way distance is measured between two points if you have to walk via streets laid out at right angles. To summarise how far the entire board is from its final position we could work out how far every tile is from its final place and add up the total number of moves.

So we now have one possible meaning of the word 'closer' in our heuristic. We examine each of the possible moves and work out the distance between the final arrangement and the one that would result if we took the move. Obviously, we should take the move that gets us closer to the final arrangement. In practice, working out the distance of the entire board may take rather too long and we can simplify things by noticing that the move that we would select is the one that produces the largest change in the distance toward the final arrangement. That is, we are not interested in the actual value of the distance, only in making it smaller. The practical result of this observation is that, as we only move one tile at a time, it is easy to find the change in the distance brought about. It is simply the change in the distance of the tile being moved from final position of that tile.

Our final and practical version of the heuristic is as follows:

(a) For each possible move
(1) work out the current distance of the tile to be moved from its home position;
(2) work out the new distance that the tile would be from its home position if it *was* moved;
(3) the difference between (1) and (2) gives the change in the overall distance if the tile was moved.
(b) Choose the move that produces the largest change toward the final position.

The heuristic approach

Altering the tile program to adopt this heuristic involves writing two new subroutines (8000 and 9000) to replace the random move generator in subroutine 6000. To run the new version of the program alter line 1060 to call subroutine 8000 instead of 6000.

```
8000 C=-5
8010 FOR I=1 TO M(P)
8020 K=VAL(MID$(M$(P),I,1))
8030 IF K=Q THEN GOTO 8060
8040 GOSUB 9000
8050 IF E>C THEN J=K:C=E
8060 NEXT I
8070 RETURN

9000 E=ABS(P-B(K)-INT((P-1)/3)*3+INT((B(K)-1)/3)*3)
9010 E=E+ABS(INT((P-1)/3)-INT((B(K)-1)/3))
9020 F=ABS(K-B(K)-INT((K-1)/3)*3+INT((B(K)-1)/3)*3)
9030 F=F+ABS(INT((K-1)/3)-INT((B(K)-1)/3))
9040 E=F-E
9050 RETURN
```

Subroutine 8000 'scans' through each possible move and calls subroutine 9000 to work out the change in distance that would be produced if the move were made. The move with the largest change is picked by line 8050. The details of the calculation in subroutine 9000 may appear difficult but all that is happening is that the city block distance is calculated once for each position (lines 9000/9010 and 9030/9040) and then the difference is taken (line 9040). Table 2.1 shows the subroutine structure of the complete program.

TABLE 2.1.

Subroutine	Description
1000	Sets up board and shuffles tile positions
2000	Prints board
3000	Sets up legal move table M$ and number of move table M
4000	Finds the current position of the 'space' and places it in P
5000	Checks for winning position, S=0 indicates that final position has been reached
7000	Performs move of tile in M(J) to M(P)
8000	Finds 'best' move
9000	Calculates evaluation function

```
8 2 3          . . .
9 5 7          . . .
6 1 4          . . .
               . . .

9 2 3          9 1 2
8 5 7          4 5 3
6 1 4          7 8 6

2 9 3          1 9 2
8 5 7          4 5 3
6 1 4          7 8 6

2 3 9          1 2 9
8 5 7          4 5 3
6 1 4          7 8 6

2 3 7          1 2 3
8 5 9          4 5 9
6 1 4          7 8 6

2 3 7          1 2 3
. . .          4 5 6
. . .          7 8 9
. . .
. . .          SOLVED IN 51     Figure 2.1
```

If you run this version of the program you might be lucky and see a solution in less than 100 moves. On the other hand you might not get a solution after thousands of moves; this is a heuristic, not an algorithm, and therefore cannot guarantee a solution. On average the program will solve one in three problems in under 100 moves (see Figure 2.1), so if you are unlucky try again with a different board.

Evaluation

Changing from making random moves to applying the heuristic involves very little extra programming but it does provide a dramatic improvement in performance. The example that the random move selection could not solve in over one hundred thousand moves is solved in 51 moves using the heuristic.

This is not to say that there are no problems with the method. Some of these difficulties are instructive in themselves and deserve further study. For example, sometimes the program 'gets stuck' repeating the same set of moves over and over again. One reason for this is that if there is a tie in the contest for 'best' move the first move in the legal move table is always taken. This could be changed, for example, to a random selection of tied moves.

The heuristic approach

Remember there is no guarantee that the heuristic will solve the problem but it is better than random selection and considerably better than no solution at all.

The heuristic used to solve the tile problem shows many of the features of heuristics applied to other problems. Its simplicity is an advantage in that it makes it easy to apply but it is worth trying to find ways of getting more out of it. Although the way that you can improve the application of a heuristic often depends on the exact nature of the problem, there is a very general method that is appropriate whenever a heuristic is being applied in a sequence of steps, each one trying to get closer to the solution. This method relies on the idea of examining the consequences of the current step on future steps.

Thinking ahead

The heuristic that we used to solve the tile game was very simple: examine each possible move and take the one that produces the maximum reduction in the distance between the current arrangement and the 'target arrangement'. This is intuitively sensible because each move tries to take us closer to the answer. However if you watch a human play the tile game you will notice that moves which make the distance greater are frequently made. What this suggests is that it is sometimes worth temporarily going away from the solution if this gains an advantage in later moves. A slightly subtler point is that it is sometimes better to choose a move that isn't the best if it leads you to a really good move later on. The conclusion from these observations is that it isn't always enough to evaluate how good the very next move is. You have to evaluate a move in terms of what moves can follow it. In other words, you have to 'look ahead'.

This sounds as though it is going to prove very difficult but in fact it is just repeated application of the methods that we have already used.

The move tree

Imagine that the game has reached the following position:

6	3	1
2	4	8
	5	7

There are two possible moves to consider. You could move either the '2' or the '5'. These can be thought of as two different 'paths' that we could take on the 'route' to a solution.

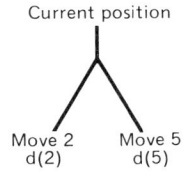

```
        Current position
              |
             / \
            /   \
        Move 2  Move 5
         d(2)    d(5)
```

Each move results in its own (possibly the same) distance from the target position and it is this that we use to choose which route we will take. (The distance after moving tile n is written as d(n) in the diagram). After taking either move we are once again confronted by a decision between a number of new moves. For example if move '5' is taken the new possible moves are '4' and '7'. Move '5' is ruled out because we don't want to move back to where we have just come from! We can add these two choices to the diagram:

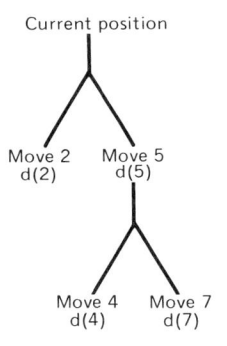

```
        Current position
              |
             / \
            /   \
        Move 2  Move 5
         d(2)    d(5)
                 / \
                /   \
            Move 4  Move 7
             d(4)    d(7)
```

The diagram of the possible moves is known as a 'move tree' because it looks like a tree drawn upside down. Each move forms a decision point or 'node' for the next stage of the game. If you were to carry on drawing nodes on the move tree you would eventually reach the target arrangement of tiles, i.e. the distance would be zero. The problem of solving the tile game can now be seen in a new light. What we are doing is searching the move tree to find a route (there may be more than one) to the final or 'terminal' node, the target arrangement. The problem of searching a tree to reach a solution is one that crops up very often in AI as a result of situations that are superficially very different.

Increasing the depth of the search

The best way of thinking about selecting moves with a certain amount of 'looking ahead' is via the move tree. Instead of evaluating each of the possible next moves, we transfer our attention to how good the subsequent moves could be. This means that for each of the moves that we are trying to decide between we must evaluate all of the moves that they lead to. Sounds easy enough but the trouble is that the number of moves that we have to consider quickly become huge. For example, if you assume that there are two choices at each node then looking one node ahead gives two moves to consider, two nodes give four moves to consider, three give eight and so on. This is not too bad in the case of the tile game, but in a game like chess, the number of possible moves at each node is more like 10 to 20 and this means that we have at least 1000 moves to search if we only look 3 ahead! Each time we look one more move ahead we are examining the next 'layer' of the tree. Searching to one move ahead is often called a 'one-ply' search and similarly searching 'n' moves ahead is referred to as an 'n-ply' search. Later in the chapter, the tile program will be extended from its current one-ply search to a two-ply search, so it is worth considering this in more detail.

Going back to the tile arrangement used earlier the two-ply tree for choosing the next move is:

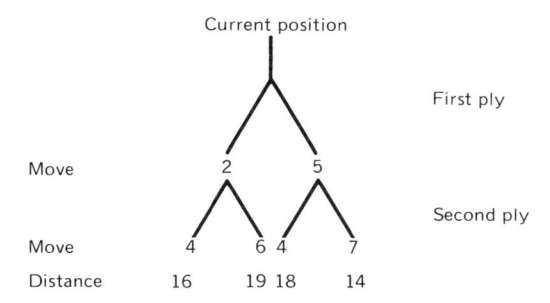

```
              Current position
                    |
                   / \
                  /   \              First ply
                 /     \
Move            2       5
               / \     / \           Second ply
              /   \   /   \
Move         4     6 4     7
Distance    16    19 18   14
```

If we take move '2' then the next move can either be '4' or '6'. Taking move '4' reduces the distance to 16 and this is smaller than 19 which results from taking move '6'. So if we take move '2' the best we can do at the next move is to reduce the distance to 16. If we take move '5' then the next move can either be '4' or '7'. Taking move '4' reduces the distance only to 18 but taking move '7' reduces it to 14. So taking move '2' we could do no better than reducing the distance to 16 at the next move but by taking move '5' we can reduce the distance to 14 at the same stage. So move '5' it is!

The distances that we associate with each of the moves i.e. 16 with '2' and 14 with '5' are not the distances that we get through moving tile '2' or tile '5' they are the distances that we could get at the next move on. As the distances actually come from further down the tree they are often called the 'backed-up distances' or, in general, the 'backed-up scores'.

After making the move of tile '5' the whole procedure starts over again with the examination a further two moves on. You might be thinking that if we know the best move for two moves ahead why not make both i.e. move tile '5' and then move tile '7'. The answer to this question is that after moving tile '5' we can evaluate move '7' using the backed-up distance from one move further down the move tree and this might prove that move '4' was better all the time! Obviously there is something a little contradictory about choosing a move on the basis of the next one being good and then not taking it and the implications of this are discussed in the next chapter.

A two-ply tile game program

Changing the one-ply program to search the move tree to a depth of two isn't too difficult. What we have to do is to examine each move in turn and calculate the backed-up distance. This is most easily done by temporarily moving the tile in question and then using the original subroutines to evaluate the subsequent possible moves. After finding the subsequent move that minimises the distance we reverse the temporary move to restore the board to its original condition before testing the next move. After all of the moves have been treated in this way, the move that gives the smallest backed-up distance is taken. The only complication is that the original tile program saved time by not calculating the total distance from the target arrangement but only the change in the distance produced by any move (subroutine 9000). So instead of trying to minimise the backed-up distance we are in fact trying to maximise the backed-up 'change in distance'.

To summarise, the final version of the program should

(1) examine each possible move in turn by temporarily making it and then examining the change in distance produced by each possible subsequent move.

(2) add the maximum change in distance produced by the subsequent move to the change in distance produced by the initial move to give the backed-up change in the distance.

(3) finally, choose the move that produces the maximum backed-up change in the distance.

The heuristic approach

This may seem very complicated but if you reason it out for yourself it should eventually make sense. What is surprising is that it is possible to implement this heuristic with only a few changes to the previous program. A revised list of subroutines can be seen in Table 2.2.

The main trouble comes from our need to temporarily make a move and evaluate it without the rest of the program 'thinking' that it is our real move. The easiest way around this problem is to introduce some new variables for keeping track of the 'real' state of the board i.e. use P1 to record the position of the hole (represented by 9) and P to record its temporary position.

The change to the original program can be seen below:

```
  65 Q1=0

 120 IF S=0 THEN GOTO 190
 130 PRINT
 140 GOSUB 8500
 150 K=J1:J=J1:P=P1:Q1=P1
 160 GOSUB 9000
 170 GOSUB 7000
 180 P1=P:M=M+1:GOSUB 2000
 185 GOTO 110

4010 IF B(I)=9 THEN P1=I

8500 C1=-5
8510 FOR Z=1 TO M(P)
8520 J0=VAL(MID$(M$(P1),Z,1))
8530 IF Q1=J0 THEN GOTO 8630
8540 J=J0:P=P1:K=J
8550 GOSUB 9000
8560 CT=E
8570 GOSUB 7000
8580 GOSUB 8000
8590 CT=CT+C
8600 IF CT>C1 THEN J1=J0:C1=CT
8610 J=P1:P=J0
8620 GOSUB 7000
8630 NEXT Z
8640 RETURN
```

There is only one new subroutine (8500) but the main program has also been modified. The main program follows the same lines as the original but now calls subroutine 8500, instead of subroutine 8000, to evaluate each of the possible moves and uses P1 to record the position of the hole and J1 as the current move. Subroutine 8500 'scans' through each of the possible moves using a FOR loop. Each move is first evaluated using subroutine 9000, the result being kept in 'CT', then the move is actually made by using subroutine 7000. Subroutine 8000 is called to evaluate all the subsequent moves in exactly the same way that it evaluated single moves in the original program. On return from subroutine 8000 'C' contains the maximum change in distance and, although it isn't actually used, 'J' contains the move that produces it. The change in distance produced by the subsequent move is added to the change in distance produced by the initial move in CT and a check is then made to see if it is larger than any found so far (stored in C1). If it is, then it becomes the largest found so far and the initial move number in J0 is recorded in J1 as the best move found so far. The temporary move made at the start of the FOR loop is then 'unmade' by using subroutine 7000 again and the next possible move is examined. At the end of subroutine 8500 the best move is in J1 and the best change that it can produce in the distance after a subsequent move is in C1.

Evaluation and suggestions

If you try this two-ply version of the tile game, you will find that it seems to make 'better' and perhaps even 'more intelligent' moves on average. However it still has an annoying tendency to get stuck in a corner repeating the same sequence of moves over and over.

TABLE 2.2.

Subroutine	Description
1000	Sets up new board and shuffles tile positions, the maximum number of moves to solve the puzzle is in M1
2000	Prints board
3000	Sets up legal move table
4000	Finds the current position of the 'space' and places it in P
5000	Checks for winning position, S=0 indicates that final position has been reached
6000	Selects a move P,J at random
7000	Performs move of tile in B(J) to B(P)
8000	Finds 'best' change in distance produced by 'second level' move
8500	Finds the 'best' backed-up change in distance for each possible move.
9000	Calculates the evaluation function for move of tile in B(K) to B(P), stores result in E

The heuristic approach

(This happens in about half of cases if the titles are shuffled more than about 50 random moves). There are three possible solutions to this problem:

(1) try to detect the 'stuck' state and then play a random move
(2) try to improve the evaluation function to avoid getting stuck
(3) increase the depth of search from two-ply to three or even four-ply.

The tile game has, however, reached the limit of its usefulness as a simple example and so any further improvements are left as a problem for you to tackle if you are interested.

Heuristics in general

In this practical example, most of the features and difficulties of a heuristic solution to a problem can be seen. In general you have to find a rule that with repeated application will tend to take you closer to your final target or goal arrangement. Although this sounds easy it is often difficult to see the problem in terms that are clear enough to allow you to find and apply a heuristic. For example, it is not always possible to measure how close you are to a solution. You can nearly always tell when you have or have not got a solution but knowing how much closer or further away from a solution a particular move takes you is often knowledge that is difficult to obtain. Indeed, in some problems, it may be difficult even to identify what constitutes a 'move'! In the tile game and other examples included in this book, the range of legal moves are set by the rules of the game. These rules tell you not only which moves are prohibited, they also give you a list of all legal moves from which you can select one that is hopefully better than the rest. The trouble with real life is that the rules are rarely simple and you may not be able to even write down all of the possible moves, let alone compare them!

Even though applying the heuristic method is often difficult, it at least gives us an alternative when the more familiar algorithmic approach fails. In short, the heuristic is an invaluable tool in human problem solving and if computers are to become thinking machines they too must employ imprecise heuristics as well as exact algorithms.

3

When heuristics meet: the strategy of competition

In the previous chapter, the idea of using a heuristic was introduced. This approach is fairly general and allows computers to be used in the solution of a wide range of problems. However, we still do not know how to deal with problems that involve 'interaction' between two solvers. In other, and more familiar, terms we have no idea how to write programs that play competitive games. For example, the tile game described in the previous chapter is fairly easy to solve using a simple heuristic that at each application takes you a little nearer to the solution. In the case of a game such a chess or draughts (checkers in the USA) this simple-minded approach would fail. The reason for this is that you might use a heuristic that at each move takes *you* a little closer to *your* solution (i.e. winning) but your opponent will attempt to undo your advantage and if possible move closer to *his* solution. It is possible to play chess using a heuristic and completely ignore the importance of any moves your opponent may make but you are unlikely to win! It is clear that to extend the heuristic method to competitive games – the simplest of which are two-person games – we have to find a way of taking into account not only the advantage resulting from the next move but how our opponent's next move wil affect it.

A simple two-person game: noughts and crosses

It is difficult to find problems that will serve as an adequate example. Most problems either turn out to be too difficult to understand quickly or too easy to present any challange to the method under discussion. Trying to find a suitable example of a two-person game is no exception. Chess is clearly too difficult and cannot be tackled with anything other than machine code.

Draughts is easier but still results in a very long program. A game that provides just the right level of difficulty is the well known 'noughts and crosses' (also called 'tic-tac-toe'). This is the most difficult two-person game that can be programmed in BASIC in a small enough number of lines to be readily understood. It also has just enough variety to illustrate some of the more advanced AI techniques. However, it does suffer from the problem that there exists a reasonably short algorithm that will result in at worse a draw and, if your opponent makes a mistake, a win. For the purpose of example, however, the algorithmic solution will be ignored. If, by the end of the chapter, you feel in need of a more complex example you could extend the programs to pay three-dimensional noughts and crosses — a real challenge not least of which is the printing of the board!

Noughts and crosses

Before going on to read the rest of this chapter, it would be a help if you could persuade someone to play a few games of noughts and crosses with you just to refresh your memory of the sort of considerations that govern the play. If you can't, then don't worry because it is not difficult to see the important points of the game. Assuming that you are playing 'O', the object of the game is to place three 'O's in a line (along a row, a column or a diagonal). Obviously, along the way to a winning position any line that could be converted into a winning line is a good thing to have. For example, two 'O's and a blank or one 'O' and two blanks in a line are good positions. However, as this is a two-person game, you cannot place your 'O' just to gain an advantage, you may have to play to block a line that your opponent is building and likewise he will play to block you.

A heuristic for noughts and crosses

A heuristic in the form of a move selector that uses an evaluation function is required to program two-person games. After the previous discussion, it should be easy to see that any evaluation function would be based on the number of lines of one and two 'O's that a move produces. In fact, if you count

$o1$ = the number of lines of 1 'O'
$o2$ = the number of lines of 2 'O's

and

$o3$ = the number of lines of 3 'O's

that a move produces you should be able to decide how good it is. But, wait a minute, what about the lines that 'X' is building up? There would be little point in making a move that resulted in a line of two 'O's if it also resulted in a line of two 'X's. (The reason for this is simple: at the next move the line of two 'X's will be converted to a line of *three* 'X's and the game will be over!) To evaluate a move it is obvious that some information about 'X's current position has to be incorporated. In the same way that 'O's position can be summarised by counting lines of 'O's, 'X's position can be summarised by counting lines of 'X's:

x1 = the number of lines of 1 'X's
x2 = the number of lines of 2 'X's

and

x3 = the number of lines of 3 'X's

To arrive at an evaluation function, we have to find some way to combine the individual measures of how things stand into a single number that increases as 'O's position gets better and decreases as 'X's position gets better. The simplest method is to add together each measure with an appropriate plus or minus sign. For example, we could use

ev = o3 − x2 + o2 − x1 + o1

which combines o3, o2 and o1 as measures of how well 'O' is doing and x2 and x1 as measures of how badly 'O' is doing. (Notice that there is no need to include x3 because if there is a line of three 'X's, the game is already over!) The trouble with this evaluation function is not difficult to spot: it ignores the relative importance of the different measures. For example, a single line of three 'O's is worth more than anything because a move that produces this result is a winning move! We can easily build in the relative importance of the measures by multiplying each of them by a constant. That is, the evaluation function is

ev = a*o3 − b*x2 + c*o2 − d*x1 + e*o1

and our only remaining problem is to establish values for a,b,c,d and e. It is very often the case that an evaluation function is a sum of a number of different measures each weighted according to how important they are. In the light of the previous discussion, a line of three 'O's should be valued above anything else so 'a' should be large enough to 'swamp' the effect of all other measures if 'o3' is 1 or more. To make things easy, we might as well settle on a value of 128 for 'a'. The values of b,c,d and e are more difficult to arrive at. Obviously, x2 is the next most important measure because a move that results in (or rather leaves) a line of two 'X's is a very *bad* move.

Hence the value of 'b' should be large but not so large that it interferes with the effect of a*o3. If 'O' has a three row it is not difficult to see that there can be at most two lines of two 'X's so as long as 2*b<a the presence of three 'O's will make itself felt over the presence of two 'X's. (If there is one line of three 'O's and two lines of two 'X's there can be no lines of one of anything to upset the evaluation!) Therefore a suitable value for 'b' is 63. By similar reasoning we can arrive at values of c=31, d=15 and k=7 giving the evaluation function its final form:

ev = 128*o3 − 63*x2 + 31*o2 − 15*x1 + 7*o1

This evaluation function can be applied to the game of noughts and crosses in the same way that the tile game evaluation function was used in the one-ply program in Chapter Two. However, before moving on to consider such a one-ply program in detail, it is worth noting that the assignment of values to the weightings a to e is often something that is a matter for trial and error. If using an evaluation function results in too many lost games then it might be time to adjust the weights used.

A one-ply noughts and crosses program

Now that we have an evaluation function it is possible to write a one-ply noughts and crosses program. Apart from the difference in details, this follows the same lines as the one-ply tile program. First 'X' (the human) is allowed to make a move and then every possible reply that 'O' can make is evaluated. The move that is selected is the one that results in the largest value of the evaluation function. That is, the move that 'O' selects is the one that 'maximises' the evaluation function.

The resulting program is not as long as you might expect.

```
  10 DIM X(4),Y(4)
  20 GOSUB 8000
  30 GOSUB 6000
  40 GOSUB 7000
  50 GOSUB 5000
  60 GOSUB 7000
  70 GOTO 30

4000 FOR K=1 TO 4:X(K)=0:Y(K)=0:NEXT K
4010 FOR L=1 TO 3
4020 S=0
4030 T=0
4040 FOR K=1 TO 3
```

```
4050 IF A(L,K)=1 THEN S=S+1
4060 IF B(L,K)=1 THEN T=T+1
4070 NEXT K
4080 IF S=0 THEN Y(T+1)=Y(T+1)+1
4090 IF T=0 THEN X(S+1)=X(S+1)+1
4100 NEXT L
4110 FOR L=1 TO 3
4120 T=0
4130 S=0
4135 FOR K=1 TO 3
4140 IF A(K,L)=1 THEN S=S+1
4150 IF B(K,L)=1 THEN T=T+1
4160 NEXT K
4170 IF S=0 THEN Y(T+1)=Y(T+1)+1
4180 IF T=0 THEN X(S+1)=X(S+1)+1
4190 NEXT L
4200 GOSUB 4300
4210 GOSUB 4400
4220 E=128*Y(4)-63*X(3)+31*Y(3)-15*X(2)+7*Y(2)
4230 RETURN

4300 T=0
4310 S=0
4320 FOR K=1 TO 3
4330 T=T+A(K,K)
4340 S=S+B(K,K)
4350 NEXT K
4360 IF S=0 THEN X(T+1)=X(T+1)+1
4370 IF T=0 THEN Y(S+1)=Y(S+1)+1
4380 RETURN

4400 T=0
4410 S=0
4420 FOR K=1 TO 3
4430 T=T+A(4-K,K)
4440 S=S+B(4-K,K)
4450 NEXT K
4460 IF S=0 THEN X(T+1)=X(T+1)+1
4470 IF T=0 THEN Y(S+1)=Y(S+1)+1
4480 RETURN

5000 M=-256
5010 FOR J=1 TO 3
5020 FOR I=1 TO 3
5030 IF A(I,J)=1 OR B(I,J)=1 THEN PRINT "OC":
     GOTO 5090
5040 B(I,J)=1
5050 GOSUB 4000
5060 PRINT E
5070 IF E>M THEN M=E:A=I:B=J
5080 B(I,J)=0
5090 NEXT I
5100 NEXT J
5110 B(A,B)=1
5120 RETURN
```

When heuristics meet: the strategy of competition

```
6000 PRINT "YOUR MOVE ";
6010 INPUT I,J
6020 A(I,J)=1
6030 RETURN

7000 FOR J=1 TO 3
7010 FOR I=1 TO 3
7020 IF A(I,J)=1 THEN PRINT "X";
7030 IF B(I,J)=1 THEN PRINT "O";
7040 IF A(I,J)+B(I,J)=0 THEN PRINT " ";
7045 PRINT ".";
7050 NEXT I
7060 PRINT
7070 NEXT J
7080 RETURN

8000 DIM A(3,3),B(3,3)
8010 GOSUB 7000
8020 RETURN
```

Once again it is written as a collection of subroutines so it should be easy for you to make use of it as a 'test bed' for any idea that you might want to try out. Table 3.1 presents its overall structure.

The main program (10–70) is simply a list of subroutine calls. Subroutine 8000 is a general set-up routine. Subroutine 6000 gets and carries out 'X's move. Subroutine 7000 prints the board. The evaluation function is calculated by subroutine 4000 which is

TABLE 3.1.

Subroutine	Description
3000	Two-ply search of the move tree
4000	Calculates evaluation function
5000	One-ply search of the move tree
6000	Gets 'X's move
7000	Prints board
8000	Sets up game

called by subroutine 5000 for each possible move that 'O' can make in reply to 'X's move. Details of the program are fairly straightforward once you know that the board is in fact represented by two different arrays 'A' and 'B'. 'A' is used to record 'X's position and 'B' records 'O's position. This use of two arrays allows both an 'X' and a 'O' to be represented by '1' and simplifies some of the calculations. Subroutine 4000 calculates the evaluation function for the board as it stands and so, to evaluate a possible move, it is necessary to actually make it before calling subroutine 4000 and then to remember to unmake it. Although there are many ways of speeding up the calculation of the evaluation function, subroutine 4000 is written to be clear rather than fast and works by counting how many of each symbol there are in every row, column and diagonal. The array 'x' is used to count how many lines of no 'X's there are (in x(1)), how many lines of exactly one 'X' there are (in x(2)) and so on up to x(4) which counts the number of lines of three 'X's there are. Similarly, the array 'y' counts the number of lines of 'O's there are. Notice that for a line to count as a line of any number of 'X's there must be no 'O's in it and vice versa. The program prints out the evaluation function for each move that it considers for general interest and prints 'oc' if a position is occupied and therefore not a potential move.

No attempt has been made to 'finish' the program (e.g. there is no check for valid moves or for the end of the game) so there is plenty of scope for improvement. However, even in its present form it is sufficient to investigate how good the evaluation function is.

Evaluation

After playing a few games against this simple program, you might be surprised at how good it is! This is rather more a reflection of how simple a game noughts and crosses is rather than how powerful the method we are using is. However, there is at least one game that the program loses and it is only by studying examples where the program fails that it can be improved. If 'X' plays 1,1 the program responds with 2,2. If then 'X' plays the rather odd move 3,3 the program responds with 3,1 resulting in the following position

```
 X |   | O
---+---+---
   | O |
---+---+---
   |   | X
```

and all is lost because X then plays 1,3. 'O' responds with 1,2 and 'X' wins by playing 2,3.

A two-ply approach: minimax

Following the arguments presented in Chapter Two, one way to improve the performance of the heuristic embodied in the evaluation function is to extend its application to a two-ply search of the move tree. The only trouble is that the next move in the move tree is determined by our opponent and is out of our control. You may feel at this point that there is nothing that we can do because, although we can evaluate our own next move, trying to consider our opponent's next move as well is impossible because we cannot either determine or dictate his next move. However, if we suppose that our opponent is reasonably competent, it is clear that he will make a move that is 'good' for his position after our move. As what is good for our opponent is bad for us, another way of saying this is that following any move that we make to improve our position, our opponent will make a move that tries to make our position as bad as possible.

What this means is that if we find a next move that results in the largest value of the evaluation function we might be disappointed to discover that our opponent's next move considerably reduces its value. Obviously faced with this situation it makes sense not to play the move that maximises the evaluation function but one that results in the largest evaluation function *after* our opponent has played his most devastating move. As his most devastating move will be the one that *minimises* our evaluation function we are in fact playing the move that maximises the evaluation function after our opponent has tried to minimise it. This strategy is known for obvious reasons as *minimax*.

The idea of maximising the minimum is not an easy one to grasp so it is worth going over the details once again but this time in terms of the move tree. A two-ply program not only has to examine every move that it might make – i.e. one level down the move tree – but also every possible reply that its opponent might make, i.e. two levels down the move tree. In the case of a non-competitive game, the program would be trying to maximise the evaluation function calculation on the position two moves ahead. But in the case of a competitive game, the second move belongs to the opponent and he will make the move that minimises the evaluation function. This situation can be represented by the following portion of the move tree

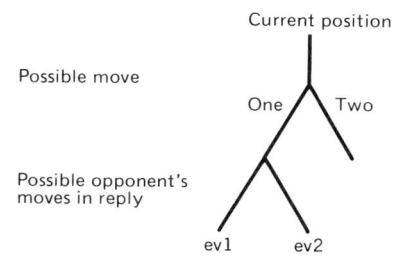

```
                    Current position
                           |
 Possible move            / \
                       One   Two
                        / \
 Possible opponent's   /   \
 moves in reply       /     \
                    ev1     ev2
```

(The real move tree even for noughts and crosses will be much larger than this!) In the situation shown, to evaluate 'possible move one' the program has to examine each of the possible replies that its opponent could make by working out the resulting evaluation functions, i.e. ev1 and ev2. Let us suppose that ev1 works out to be 5 and ev2 10. It is obvious that the opponent will choose the first move in reply (it minimises the program's evaluation function). So, if the program chooses move one the result will be ev1 (i.e. 5) at the next move. Using the same terminology introduced to deal with deeper exploration of the move trees produced by the tile game, ev1 is the 'backed-up' value of the evaluation function and the program selects the move that *maximises* the backed-up value.

A BASIC two-ply minimax program

To produce a BASIC program that implements this two-ply minimax search, it is only necessary to rewrite the search subroutine and the evaluation function subroutine. The new versions of these subroutines are presented below.

```
    50 GOSUB 3000

  3000 G=-255
  3010 FOR J=1 TO 3
  3020 FOR I=1 TO 3
  3030 IF A(I,J)=1 OR B(I,J)=1 THEN PRINT "OC";
       GOTO 3180
  3040 B(I,J)=1
  3050 D=255
  3060 FOR M=1 TO 3
  3070 FOR N=1 TO 3
  3080 IF A(M,N)=1 OR B(M,N)=1 THEN GOTO 3130
  3090 A(M,N)=1
  3100 GOSUB 4000
  3110 IF E<D THEN D=E
  3120 A(M,N)=0
  3130 NEXT N
  3140 NEXT M
  3150 PRINT D
  3160 IF D>G THEN G=D:A=I:B=J
  3170 B(I,J)=0
  3180 NEXT I
  3190 NEXT J
  3200 B(A,B)=1
  3210 RETURN

  4220 E=256*Y(4)-128*X(4)-63*X(3)+31*Y(3)-
       15*X(2)+7*Y(2)
  4230 F=128*X(4)-63*Y(3)+31*X(3)-15*Y(2)+7*X(2)
  4240 RETURN
```

If you've followed the discussion of the one-ply program and the ideas involved in the minimax search the workings of this program should become clear after a little study. Subroutine 3000 takes each possible move in turn and evaluates it by making each possible reply and then calling subroutine 4000 to calculate the evaluation function. The backed-up score is found by storing the minimum result of subroutine 4000 in 'd'. This is then compared to the current largest value of the backed up score stored in 'g'. In this way the move that has the largest backed-up score is found. Notice that, as subroutine 4000 still calculates the evaluation function on the board as it actually stands, it is necessary first to make each possible move, call subroutine 4000 to evaluate it and then remember to unmake it to restore the board to its original condition. The only other point of any importance is the inclusion of a count of the number of lines of three 'X's. In the one-ply program a line of three 'X's could never be present for the evaluation function to report on because the game would have ended at an earlier move! However, in the two-ply program looking two moves ahead it is possible for it to foresee such a disaster and so the evaluation function must be modified to reflect the importance of *not* making a move that results in a line of three 'X's at the opponent's next move!

Evaluating the two-ply program

The first thing that should strike you about the two-ply program is that it is slow. This is partly a reflection of the fact that, for the sake of clarity, no attempt has been made to save time in the BASIC program. However, it is also a reflection of the fact that the amount of work required for a two-ply search is greater. This is an observation that is at the root of most of the problems encountered in writing game-playing programs. Even a poor evaluation function will improve when used further down the move tree but the amount of calculation involved grows to astronomical proportions! The question of whether the extra work involved in a two-ply search is worth it is quickly (or, should I say, slowly) answered by playing the game that the one-ply program loses. In this case the two-ply program finds a way to avoid certain defeat but I leave it to you to discover why.

Beyond noughts and crosses

The game of noughts and crosses has served us well as an example but its usefulness is exhausted at the two-ply program. It simply isn't difficult enough to warrant a deeper evaluation and hence more programming. (However, it will be used once more in the next chapter as an example of the slightly different problem of writing a program that *learns* to play a game.) To see how the subject of programs that play competitive games develops, it is necessary to consider chess or draughts. For a program to play either of these games at all, it is necessary for it to examine the move tree to a depth of four or more moves on. To examine the entire move tree to this depth requires many hours (even if the program is written in machine code) so most of the programming effort goes into finding ways of ignoring moves that are obviously not worth making. This discarding of parts of the move tree is often referred to as 'pruning' and unfortunately it is beyond the scope of this book to go into its details.

Other areas of competitive game-playing programs that are of interest include special methods for playing opening and end games. In the case of noughts and crosses, the first move made by 'O' is either the top left hand corner or the centre depending on which is unoccupied. This observation can be used to speed up the program by writing a special 'first move' subroutine. This is an example of an 'opening game' routine. In the case of chess, it is usual to keep the first few moves of 'classical' openings stored in memory to take the game to a point where the evaluation function can take over. In the same way, there are often special strategies for ending a game and these too are often built into game-playing programs to take over from the evaluation function when the game has reached a point where it can be easily won.

Another area that can be pursued is the improvement of the evaluation function as the program plays. This magical sounding result can be achieved by noticing that the backed-up score tell us how good the move is a after a number of further moves. The value of the function calculated on the move itself should also reflect how good the move is but without the advantage of looking further down the tree. Obviously a good evaluation function will tend to give roughly the same answer when applied one move ahead as when applied n-moves ahead to give the backed-up value. (If this is the case you can get nearly as good results without searching as deep!) If this is not the case then the program can try to improve the quality of the evaluation function by adjusting the sizes of the constants used to define it. In this way the program can 'learn' to do better.

Competitive heuristics

It is easy to forget how difficult playing chess really is and to minimise the achievment involved in developing chess playing programs that can challenge human players. At the moment, there is no chess program that can beat the best human chess players but even the sort of program that you buy for a home computer can put up a fairly good performance. In other words, even these humble micros are capable of a level of problem solving that can match a human opponent. In this short introduction to the ideas involved in using heuristics against an opponent we have encountered most of the ideas involved in writing programs that come close to being as good as humans at a particular range of supposedly intelligent tasks.

4
Thinking and reasoning: expert systems

So far, the two classical AI problems that we have looked at – the tile game and noughts and crosses – might lead you to the conclusion that artificial intelligence seems to be about writing programs that replicate a very small part of human behaviour. For, although game playing may be a very general topic, once you concentrate on a particular game it seems very quickly necessary to develop special theories and methods. However the main problem of AI is about replicating the most general sort of mental activity – thinking.

To a certain extent, programs that play games such as chess are attempts at carrying out tasks that humans would say need 'thought'. The trouble is that once you know how such programs work it is difficult to believe that they play in the same way that humans do. Do grand masters really analyse chess problems six to ten moves ahead? Aren't chess programs simply using the computer's speed to do a 'brute force' analysis of the game? In the same way that it is clear that chess programs are not playing chess in the same way that humans do, many AI programs seem to achieve roughly the same result as a human but by methods that seem very different. It is important to realise that whenever you come to understand the way that an AI program works you are bound to think that its operation is essentially simple – anything you understand seems simple.

All this seems to lead to the conclusion that perhaps the AI programs that we have looked at so far are simply clever programs rather than intelligent programs! This is in part true but it does ignore some important points. The human brain is a very complicated device and it is quite capable of carrying out a large number of very simple operations at the same time. It is, therefore, quite possible that human intelligence is the result of many simple operations carried out simultaneously or repeatedly. What this means for our study of artificial intelligence is that we may one day know exactly how a human does something but have no way of using this knowledge to write a program because no digital computer could run it in a reasonable time. In other words, the choice may be to do it as a human does it, and not have a practical program or take advantage of the particular talent of the digital computer, or do it in a non-human way. So, in the case of chess playing, it is likely that human players do look a number of moves ahead, but they do not examine all the possible moves. Instead they use a heuristic to 'prune' the move tree down to a manageable size. Most computer chess programs examine more of the moves in the move tree and use a simple pruning alogrithm (rather than heuristic) to find a good move. In this way a computer will very often come up with a move that is, to a human, not part of any playing 'strategy'. Because of this, good human chess players tend to identify computer play as non-human, but this may not be a difference in kind just a difference in emphasis.

So, do computer chess programs in any sense 'think' about the game they are playing? To a certain extent the answer to this question depends on how cautiously you use the word 'think'. The chess program is using some of the methods that a human probably uses; weighing up moves, examining some parts of the move tree etc. However, to make the chess program practical it uses the unique advantages of the digital computer to do arithmetic and search the move tree fully to a given depth. In my opinion, chess programs do not think about chess but they do share some things in common with human players.

It is the same story with other AI programs; they use some human methods but combine them with methods that suit a computer. It may be that one day programs will be written that rely solely on human methods but I feel that this is unlikely in the near future. For the time being, we will write programs that play chess or solve problems using a certain amount of cleverness mixed with brute force.

This is not to say that we cannot write programs that give the appearance of thinking. In the same way that we write chess programs that play chess to master level, it is quite possible to write programs in specific areas that 'think' and solve problems as well as experts.

A general problem solver

It is not difficult to write a program that solves problems of a specific type. For example, you could write a program that would prove mathematical theorems. Indeed, reseachers in AI have written programs that 'reason' about areas of mathematics so well that they occasionally find a better proof of a known theorem or even find and prove a theorem that was previously unknown. In this sense, we can say that AI programs have already surpassed man's intelligence! Of course, if you take a maths theorem-proving program and ask it something unconnected with mathematics, you won't get a reasonable response! The program works within a very small 'world' and it cannot move outside to consider anything else. However, in the early days of AI research, it was shown that a general-purpose logical reasoning program could be written. All you had to do was give it a description of the 'world' that it had to reason about and off it would go, solving logical problems with no trouble.

Humans solving problems

Computers reason using exact logic and this is why they are so good at proving mathematical theorems. However, humans rarely think logically in this sense unless they are forced to by the nature of the problem. This is not to say that humans think illogically! What tends to happen is that a human will not analyse the situation in minute detail but try to draw on past experience. He or she will try to match some detail of the problem with something seen in the past. In other words, use is made of a wide-ranging knowledge of the way that the world works, knowledge that is generally not included in programs that reason logically.

If this is the case then to construct programs that reason about things in the way that humans do, we should first look at the representation of knowledge inside a computer. Computers are thought to be good at collecting and storing vast amounts of information and indeed this is true, but they store it in a very simple way. A computer's collection of facts is more like the way that an encyclopedia 'remembers' things rather than the way a human remembers. For example, a collection of facts is useless unless you know what the 'consequences' of a fact are. If you are trying to decide what the weather will be, both you and the computer might know that the sky is black and full of clouds but only you can deduce that this means that it is likely to rain. In other words, you know the (possible) consequences of a black, cloud-filled sky, the computer does not!

It is not difficult to think of ways of storing information along with its consequences as a collection of rules. For example, the weather 'knowledge' could be stored inside a computer as

IF black cloudy sky THEN high possibility of rain

Thinking and reasoning: expert systems

In general, a piece of knowledge can be represented by a list of conditions and a list of consequences. For example,

IF black clouds,high humidity,summer THEN thunder storm

might be a statement of what we know about thunder storms! The commas between each condition should be read as AND because each of the conditions has to apply before we are willing to reach the conclusion with a degree of confidence. Notice that although we are using IF...THEN, which is so familiar from programming, this use is different. In this case, IF...THEN isn't an instruction to do something if something else is true, it is a statement of the relationship between different facts.

If you wanted to construct a program that would use such rules to solve problems then all you would do is to collect as many rules as possible, in other words build a 'rule data base' and, then, to find out the meaning or consequence of a set of conditions, simply search the data base for rules with the same conditions. There may be more than one rule for any particular set of conditions. For example, if you knew that there was a black sky you might search and find both of the IF...THEN weather rules given above. The predicted consequences would be rain by the first rule and possibly a thunder storm from the second. To find out which was more likely you would have to supply more information.

Programs of this sort are usually referred to as 'knowledge-based expert systems' and they are receiving a great deal of attention from the community and the general public at the moment as the best thing that AI has ever produced. You now know that such programs are not at all complicated! The main problem with any expert system is the initial collection of the rules that form the data base. This is usually accomplished by working with a human expert and trying to find out what rules he uses.

Rather than continue with theory and explanation it is easier and more instructive to proceed straight to a simple BASIC expert system.

The Aardvark program

All this talk of knowledge rules and expert systems may seem convincing, but does it work? To demonstrate how powerful the idea is, the program given below will learn to become an expert on types of animals. The reason why types of animal has been used is that this particular program has a long history in one form or another and has always been presented with an animal data base. However, since the program learns the data rather than having it already built-in you could use it in other areas, such as fault diagnosis, just by changing the first question asked. The reason that this is a very simple expert system is that it uses rules of the sort

IF list of animal characteristics THEN it is an 'animal name'

For example, you might have the rule

IF it has feathers, is a predator THEN it is an eagle

To make finding the correct rule easy and to make the addition and modification of existing rules possible all of the rules are

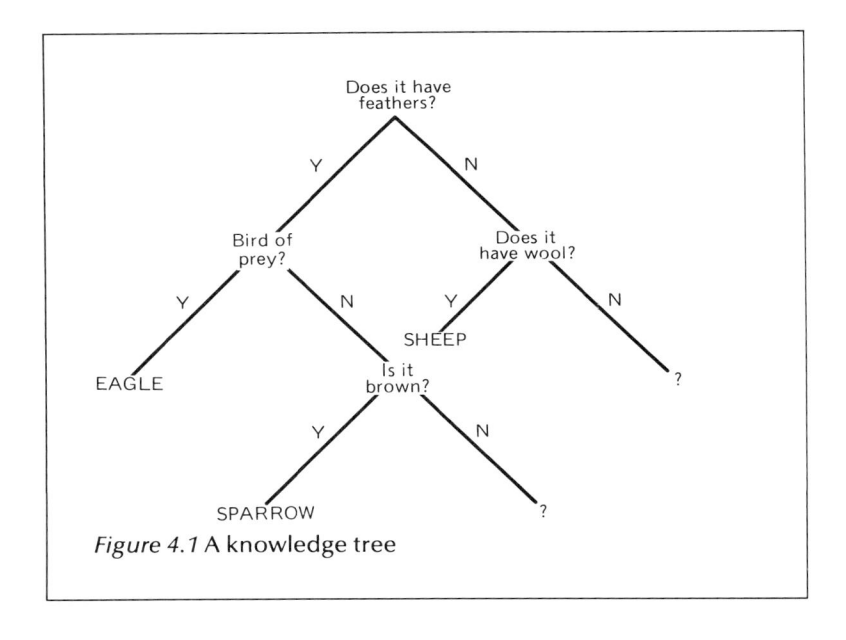

Figure 4.1 A knowledge tree

represented by a tree. The use of a tree is not essential to the method but it does have many practical advantages and seems to fit quite naturally into the program.

To see how a tree can be used to represent a number of rules, look at Figure 4.1. Starting from the first question "does it have feathers", you can work your way down the tree answering the questions until you come to an animal's name. Each time you answer a question you take the branch of the tree that corresponds to the answer, i.e. the lefthand branch for "yes" and righthand

Thinking and reasoning: expert systems

branch for "no" and ask the next question you meet. For example, if the answer to "does it have feathers" is "no" then the next question is "does it have wool". If the answer to this question is "yes" then the animal is a sheep. The rules that are contained in this tree are

  IF feathers,predator THEN eagle
  IF feathers,not predator, brown THEN sparrow
  IF not feathers,wool THEN sheep

You should be able to see that each of these rules is represented in the tree by the path that you have to take to get to the animal's name. The advantage of storing the rules in this form is that you can match the conditions against the rules one at a time rather than all together. It also provides a way of asking the user to supply information when it is necessary rather than all at once.

This is all very well but how do the rules and the tree structure get there in the first place? The answer is that every time the Aardvark program reaches a "?" in the tree structure, it doesn't know what the animal is. To put this to rights and gain some information, it asks the user what the animal is called and for a question that it can ask next time to identify the animal. Once it has this information, it inserts it into the tree structure for later use. For example, suppose after asking a number of questions the program finds itself at the "?" following the "is it brown" question. It then asks the user "what is the animal" to be told that it is a seagull and the question it should ask is "is it a sea bird". The result is that the new question replaces the question mark and the "yes" branch of the new part of the tree leads to "seagull" and the "no" branch to yet another question mark.

There is one other way that the Aardvark program can learn and that is by getting the answer wrong! If it follows a path down the tree and arrives at the answer "sparrow" only to be informed by the user that the animal is in fact a "wren" then it can avoid this mistake a second time by asking the user for another question to ask to tell the difference between the two birds. For example, if the question is "is it the smallest brown British bird" then the "wren" would be on the yes branch and the "sparrow" on the no branch. The question itself would of course replace the entry "sparrow" in the original tree. In this way, the tree 'grows' and modifies itself to reflect what you tell it about animals. You will have to try it for yourselves to see just how quickly it learns but it is great fun to use!

The program is written in a standard Microsoft BASIC, as before, and should run on almost any machine without modification apart from the ZX81 and the Spectrum which will require some slight changes to the string handling.

```
 10 PRINT "AARDVARK"
 20 PRINT "YOU THINK OF AN ANIMAL AND"
 30 PRINT "I WILL GUESS IT -"
 40 PRINT "ANSWER EACH QUESTION WITH"
 50 PRINT "YES OR NO"
 60 PRINT
 70 GOSUB 1000

 100 GOSUB 2000
 110 PRINT
 120 PRINT "THINK OF A NEW ANIMAL - "
 130 PRINT
 140 GOTO 100

1000 DIM Q$(20),R(20),L(20),N$(20)
1010 Q$(1)="DOES IT HAVE FEATHERS"
1020 D=1
1030 R(1)=0
1040 L(1)=0
1050 N=0
1060 Q=1
1070 RETURN

2000 X=1
2010 GOSUB 3000
2020 IF A$="Y" AND R(X)=0 THEN GOTO 4000
2030 IF A$="N" AND L(X)=0 THEN GOTO 4000
2040 IF A$="Y" AND R(X)<0 THEN A=-R(X):GOTO 5000
2050 IF A$="N" AND L(X)<0 THEN A=-L(X):GOTO 5000
2060 IF A$="Y" THEN X=R(X)
2070 IF A$="N" THEN X=L(X)
2080 GOTO 2010

3000 PRINT Q$(X)
3010 INPUT A$
3020 A$=LEFT$(A$,1)
3030 IF A$="Y" OR A$="N" THEN RETURN
3040 PRINT "I DO NOT UNDERSTAND YOUR ANSWER"
3050 PRINT "PLEASE ANSWER YES OR NO TO MY"
3060 PRINT "QUESTIONS - THANK YOU"
3070 PRINT
3080 GOTO 3000

4000 PRINT "I DO NOT KNOW THE ANIMAL"
4010 PRINT "THAT YOU ARE THINKING OF"
4020 PRINT "WHAT IS IT CALLED "
4030 INPUT B$
4040 PRINT
4050 PRINT "WHAT EXTRA QUESTION CAN I ASK"
4060 PRINT "TO DISTINGUISH THIS NEW ANIMAL"
4070 INPUT C$
4080 N=N+1
4090 N$(N)=B$
4100 Q=Q+1
```

Thinking and reasoning: expert systems

```
4110 Q$(Q)=C$
4120 IF A$="Y" THEN R(X)=D+1 ELSE L(X)=D+1
4130 PRINT "FOR A ";B$
4140 PRINT "WHAT IS THE ANSWER TO"
4150 PRINT C$
4160 INPUT D$
4170 D$=LEFT$(D$,1)
4180 IF D$="Y" OR D$="N" THEN GOTO 4300
4190 PRINT "ANSWER YES OR NO PLEASE"
4200 GOTO 4130
4300 D=D+1
4310 IF D$="Y" THEN R(D)=-N:L(D)=0
4320 IF D$="N" THEN L(D)=-N:R(D)=0
4330 RETURN

5000 PRINT "IS IT A ";N$(A);
5010 INPUT B$
5020 IF LEFT$(B$,1)="N" THEN GOTO 6000
5030 IF LEFT$(B$,1)<>"Y" THEN PRINT "ANSWER
     YES OR NO PLEASE":GOTO 5000
5040 PRINT "I THOUGHT SO !!"
5050 PRINT
5060 RETURN

6000 PRINT "I GIVE UP !"
6010 INPUT "WHAT IS IT",B$
6020 PRINT "WHAT QUESTION WOULD TELL"
6030 PRINT "THE DIFFERENCE BETWEEN A ";N$(A)
6040 PRINT "AND YOUR ";B$
6050 INPUT C$
6060 Q=Q+1
6070 Q$(Q)=C$
6080 N=N+1
6090 N$(N)=B$
6100 IF A$="Y" THEN R(X)=Q ELSE L(X)=Q
6110 D=D+1
6120 PRINT "FOR A ";B$
6130 PRINT "WHAT IS THE ANSWER TO"
6140 PRINT C$
6150 INPUT D$
6160 D$=LEFT$(D$,1)
6170 IF D$="Y" THEN R(D)=-N:L(D)=-A
6180 IF D$="N" THEN L(D)=-N:R(D)=-A
6190 PRINT
6200 RETURN
```

The details of the program are not difficult to understand. The subroutine structure is

   10   Introductory instruction
  100   Main program loop – once round per animal
 1000   Initialisation subroutine
 2000   Ask question and process answer

3000 Answer input routine
4000 Don't know animal, so get new animal and question
5000 Report animal found and check correct
6000 Incorrect guess so get new animal and question

The only other information that it is important to know is that the tree structure is represented by two arrays, L and R, corresponding to the left and right branch of the tree, following each question. If you reach an element of whether the L or the R array that contains zero then you have reached the end of the tree and don't know what the animal is. If you reach an element of either array that contains a negative number you have found a possible candidate for the animal. The names of the animals are stored in the array N$ and the index of the animal that you have found is stored in the L or R array as a negative number. So if you find that L(X) is negative the animal's name is in N$(−L(X)). If, however, the value stored in R or L is positive and not zero then this is the index of the next question you should ask and the index of the next element of either R or L you should look at as a result of the answer to the question. Finally, the questions are stored in the array Q$.

The tree starts off with one question and no animal names stored. So Q$(1) contains the question and R(1) and L(1) both contain zero (you can think of zero as standing for the question mark in the tree diagram in Figure 4.1.) If the answer to the first question is "yes" then R(1) is examined and as it is zero the program asks for an animal name and a new question. The new name is stored in N$(1) and the question in Q$(2). R(1) is changed to 2 so that question Q$(2) will be asked following a "yes" answer to question 1 and R(2) and L(2) are changed so that one of them holds −1 to indicate that the animal's name is in N$(1) and the other is set to zero to indicate that yet another question and name is needed. Figure 4.2 gives a sample of Aardvarks output.

More work on Aardvark

Aardvark is a simple program but is does work out a conclusion from a set of conditions and it does learn from both its ignorance and its mistakes. The way in which it grows the knowledge tree is haphazard but it is flexible. For example, an animal can appear more than once in the tree to allow for different sets of conditions that 'define' it. The biggest problem is that the order that the questions are asked is purely governed by the order that they are learned and this is usually not the best order. If a human was playing Aardvark, the first question would be chosen in such a way as to provide the maximum information. For example, by asking

Thinking and reasoning: expert systems

```
AARDVARK
YOU THINK OF AN ANIMAL AND
I WILL GUESS IT -
ANSWER EACH QUESTION WITH
YES OR NO

DOES IT HAVE FEATHERS
? no
I DO NOT KNOW THE ANIMAL
THAT YOU ARE THINKING OF
WHAT IS IT CALLED
? dog

WHAT EXTRA QUESTION CAN I ASK
TO DISTINGUISH THIS NEW ANIMAL
? does it bark
FOR A DOG
WHAT IS THE ANSWER TO
DOES IT BARK
? yes

THINK OF A NEW ANIMAL

DOES IT HAVE FEATHERS
? no
DOES IT BARK
? no

I DO NOT KNOW THE ANIMAL
THAT YOU ARE THINKING OF
WHAT IS IT CALLED
? cow

WHAT EXTRA QUESTION CAN I ASK
TO DISTINGUISH THIS NEW ANIMAL
? does it eat grass
FOR A COW
WHAT IS THE ANSWER TO
DOES IT EAT GRASS
? yes

THINK OF A NEW ANIMAL

DOES IT HAVE FEATHERS
?no
DOES IT BARK
? no
DOES IT EAT GRASS
? yes
IS IT A COW ? n
I GIVE UP!
WHAT IS IT ? sheep
WHAT QUESTION WOULD TELL
THE DIFFERENCE BETWEEN A COW
AND YOUR SHEEP
? does it provide wool
FOR A SHEEP
WHAT IS THE ANSWER TO
DOES IT PROVIDE WOOL
? yes
```

Figure 4.2 Sample of Aardvark's output. For clarity, the user's responses are given in lowercase letters "does it have feathers", you can immediately narrow down the rest of the search into one of the two categories: birds or non-birds. It would be possible to add a section to the program that will examine the tree and find the best arrangement for the questions but this is beyond the scope of this book.

As suggested earlier, by changing the first question in Aardvark to something else like "is the fault electrical", the program could be turned into a fault finder. Of course, naming the fault is only part of the solution. You also should store instructions about what to do along with the name. Some other suggestions for facilities that you might like to add to Aardvark are

add a routine to save and read in an existing tree
find a way of printing the entire tree for analysis
allow the user to ask for a description of any animal in the tree

Aardvark is not as sophisticated as a fully commercial expert system. In particular, it doesn't allow for the possibility that its conclusions may be uncertain.

On being over-confident

The idea of a computer program that reasons by using rules of the IF condition THEN conclusion type seems very natural and promising until you start to consider the sort of judgments humans make. It is not very often that a decision can be made with absolute certainty. It is more often the case that we say things like "I think the trouble might be" or "It could be ..." than we say "I know" or "It is". So far, all the IF...THEN rules that we have considered have assumed that the answer to any question was known with absolute certainty and that the presence of any given condition was always an absolute sign that the conclusion should be drawn. It is certainly clear that this is not always so! A component of human reasoning that we have ignored so far is uncertainty.

There are two ways of dealing with uncertainty in reasoning. The first is traditional and based on probability. The second is fairly new and not so well developed so there is scope for experimentation. However, it is important to realise that there are two different sorts of uncertainty that occur in reasoning. The first is just not being sure of the condition. For example, you might have caught sight of an animal only for a moment and not be sure if it had a tail or not. This is being uncertain of the evidence and is generally easy to deal with. The second type of uncertainty is where the evidence is quite clear cut, i.e. you are sure of the facts, but there is no certain connection between what you know and the conclusion that you draw. For example, you may be sure that the weather is humid but this only increases the chances that there will be a thunder storm. This form of uncertainty is known as 'uncertainty in inference' and it cannot be ignored as a component of reasoning.

Probability

We are all familiar with the idea of the probability of something happening. Even so, most of us have only an intuitive idea that the higher the probability the more likely the thing is to happen. A probability of zero corresponds to the certain knowledge that an event will not happen and a probability of one corresponds to the certain knowledge that an event will happen. So probabilities of zero and one correspond to certainty and values in between correspond to uncertainty. (You might notice the similarity here between probability and Boolean logic). The best interpretation that we have of probability is in terms of the number of times something happens. For example, if you toss an unbiased coin a great many times it will come up heads roughly half of them. In this sense we can say that the statement 'the probability of getting heads is 0.5' is a statement about what proportion of heads we would expect to see in a large number of throws. This idea generalises quite simply to an interpretation of the probability of other events as the proportion of the time that they occur in the long run.

This all sounds like a good solid, realistic way to understand probability and it is generally considered to be the best. However consider the situation where you are asked to say how likely something is to be true or false. In this case it is difficult to see how the idea of the number of times something is true or false in the long run can be used as an interpretation of the probability. For example, "what do you reckon the probability is that life exists on other planets?" is a question that you might be prepared to answer but it is difficult to see how the probability that you give as an answer can be interpreted as the number of times you are likely to be right in the long run. Even the wildest imagination will find it difficult to cope with more than one universe in which to repeat the event! There are many ways round this difficulty but the easiest is to abandon the direct interpretation of probability as an indication of how often something would occur. Of course, once you do this you can only use probability as a vague measure of how certain you are of something and this cannot be verified in the same way as the proportion of times that an event happens; it is in this sense subjective. The trouble is that once you abandon the physical meaning of probability, there is nothing to recommend it over and above any other measure of uncertainty!

Rather than use probability you could choose to work with another measure of uncertainty and a different set of rules for combining such measures and, because the whole thing is subjective, no one could argue with you! The point is that while probability may be just right for summarising our uncertainty about some events in the world, it isn't necessarily the best way of summarising the way humans 'feel' uncertain about something. You may be a little sceptical about using something other than probability, so a little later in this chapter one of the alternatives, fuzzy logic is described.

The laws of uncertain thought?

Even though there are philosophical problems with using probability in some areas of human knowledge and reasoning, it is still the system that we are most used to. For this reason, it is worth examining how probability could be added to the sort of expert system represented by Aardvark. To be able to do this, we need to look at a little of the theory of probability. The probability of an event x is normally written as $P(x)$ which should be read as a shorthand for 'the probability of x'. For example, $P(\text{heads,})$ is the probability of getting heads when a coin is spun, which is 0.5 if the coin is unbiased. A slightly more complicated but very useful idea is that of 'conditional probability'. This is usually written as $P(A|B)$ and is read as 'the probability that A will happen given B has happened'. (You will find the rest of this chapter easier to read if you get into the habit of reading symbols like $P(A|B)$ as 'the probability of A given B', i.e. read P as 'the probability' and the vertical bar as 'given'.) So for example, $P(\text{rain})$ is just the probability of rain but $P(\text{rain}|\text{dark clouds present})$ is the probability of rain given that we already know that there are dark clouds in the sky. In other words, a conditional probability is the probability of something *after* including any knowledge that we might already have.

You should be able to see that conditional probabilities are something like uncertain IF...THEN rules. If you are certain about things, then you write rules such as

IF dark clouds in sky THEN rain

whereas if you are admitting the existence of uncertainty then you would use the rule

$P(\text{rain this afternoon}|\text{dark clouds}) = 0.9$

which gives a reasonable indication of how certain you are that IF dark clouds THEN rain this afternoon.

Thinking and reasoning: expert systems

Conditional probabilities are just a little more difficult to use than indicated above because of the problem of finding out the actual values to be used. There is, however, a very useful mathematical connection between $P(A|B)$ and $P(B|A)$:

$$P(A|B) = \frac{P(B|A)P(A)}{P(B)}$$

Using this simple equation, we can work out $P(\text{rain}|\text{black clouds})$ from a knowledge of $P(\text{black clouds}|\text{rain})$

$$P(\text{rain}|\text{black clouds}) = \frac{P(\text{black clouds}|\text{rain})P(\text{rain})}{P(\text{black clouds})}$$

As $P(\text{black clouds}|\text{rain})$ can be considered to be 1 (i.e. whenever it rains there are *always* black clouds) this gives

$$P(\text{rain}|\text{black clouds}) = \frac{P(\text{rain})}{P(\text{black clouds})}$$

Which makes a great deal of sense if you think about the meaning of this final equation. $P(\text{rain})$ is just the proportion of time that it rains and $P(\text{black clouds})$ is just the proportion of the time that black clouds occur whether it rains or not!

This idea of changing $P(B|A)$ into $P(A|B)$ is not only practically useful, it forms the basis of the standard method of reasoning with probability. The equation that connects $P(B|A)$ with $P(A|B)$ is called Bayes' Theorem after the Reverand Thomas Bayes who first derived it and its use in reasoning is often referred to as Bayesean inference. Suppose you were sitting in a room without any window and absolutely no knowledge of what the weather might be doing. Your best estimate of the chance of it raining outside would be simply $P(\text{rain})$. That is, simply the proportion of the time that it normally rains. In the sense $P(\text{rain})$ summarises how much you believe that it is raining if you have no other knowledge. If you were given the information that if there were black clouds in the sky outside you would have to revise your belief in rain to take this information into account. Using

$$P(\text{rain}|\text{dark clouds}) = \frac{P(\text{dark clouds}|\text{rain})\,P(\text{rain})}{P(\text{dark clouds})}$$

you can change what you believed, $P(\text{rain})$, before the extra information into your new belief, $P(\text{rain}|\text{dark clouds})$. If some more information comes into your isolated room, e.g. a clap of thunder was heard, you could use the same method to update what you believed once again!

$$P(\text{rain}|\text{thunder, dark clouds}) = \frac{P(\text{thunder}|\text{rain})\, P(\text{rain}|\text{dark clouds})}{P(\text{thunder})}$$

and so on. Each new piece of information would be used to change what you already believed into your new belief. To do this all you have to do is to multiply the probability that represents your old belief by a constant which indicates how much evidence the new information provides for or against the belief. In the case of rain and thunder for example, the constant is $P(\text{thunder}|\text{rain})/P(\text{thunder})$. In some extreme cases, the evidence may be so overwhelming that your belief becomes a certainty. For example, if dark clouds *never* occurred without rain and rain *never* occurred with dark clouds (by the way, I know that both these propositions are not true!) then $P(\text{dark clouds}|\text{rain})$ would be 1 and $P(\text{dark clouds})$ would be the same as $P(\text{rain})$ as they would always occur together. Using these in the previous equation gives

$$P(\text{rain}|\text{dark clouds}) = \frac{1}{P(\text{rain})} P(\text{rain})$$
$$= 1$$

which at least shows that things work according to common sense.

You should be able to see that this method could be added to Aardvark to produce an expert system that could cope with uncertain IF...THEN rules. At each decision point in the tree, you would supply a new piece of information which could be used to update the probability of each conclusion. Suppose the knowledge tree consisted of only three animals: lion, tiger and cheetah. At the start of the program the 'belief' that the computer had that each of the animals was the one you had thought of would be simply $P(\text{lion})$, $P(\text{tiger})$, $P(\text{cheetah})$. (If you find this difficult to understand compare it with the previous example of weather forecasting from the isolated room, where in the absence of any information your belief that it was going to rain was $P(\text{rain})$.) Each time you answer a question or supply some information the program would update its belief in each animal being the correct solution. For example, telling the program that the animal could run fast wouldn't make the program decide that your animal was a cheetah because lions and tigers can also run quite fast! Instead it would use this information to increase the probability that you had thought of a cheetah and reduce the probabilities of it being a lion or a tiger. However, if you gave it some information that made the probability of it being one of the animals equal 1, it would immediately give you its decision. In many cases, however, even after you had supplied it with everything that you knew about the animal it would still not be able to tell you certainly what the answer was. Instead it would have to report the animal with the highest probability or even a number of very probable animals.

Obviously, this idea can be generalised to more serious and useful applications. For example, in the case of diagnosing car faults, the expert system would start off with a list of possible faults and their probabilities. It would also contain a number of probability rules such as P(carburettor fault|smell of petrol)=0.8 or P(hole in petrol tank|smell of petrol)=0.9, which would be used to update the initial probabilities as the evidence was presented to the program. The final results would not necessarily be a clear cut diagnosis but instead might be a list of possible faults and how likely they were.

A BASIC program that uses uncertain inference is not given here simply because the success of such a program depends very much on how well the knowledge base is constructed. It takes a great deal of time to produce a good expert system but the principles by which it operates are not difficult to understand.

Uncertain evidence

The previous section discussed the most difficult aspect of uncertainty but hasn't really given a clue as to what to do when you are uncertain about the evidence. The answer is surprisingly simple and surprisingly unsatisfactory. If you include in an expert system a supplementary question such as, "How sure are you (on a scale 0 to 1) of your last answer ?" then you will collect estimates of the certainty of each piece of information that you are going to base your conclusion on. If you treat these estimates as probabilities then the correct way of using them to estimate the uncertainty in your conclusion is very complicated and depends on knowing the relationships that exist between the different pieces of information. As these relationships are generally unknown the usual assumption is that they are non-existent and this implies that the correct estimate of the uncertainty of the conclusion should be obtained by multiplying all the probabilities together. (This is because of a theorem in probability that says that if a number of events are independent the probability of them all happening is the product of their individual probabilities.) This sounds very reasonable until you notice that 0.5 times 0.5 is rather small and even if you start out with large certainties, such as 0.9, the final certainty of the conclusion will be very small if you have very much evidence!

Multiplying probabilities gives a very conservative estimate of the certainty of the conclusion because we are ignoring the relationships between the evidence!

There is no really acceptable solution to this problem and most expert systems invent their own way of dealing with it. However there is one method that is appealing because it fits in with the topic of our next section, fuzzy logic. Instead of multiplying the certainties together the certainty of the conclusion is estimated by taking the minimum of the certainties.

Alternatives to probability: fuzzy logic

You may have noticed that although we started out by being exact and using probabilities in precise ways, the section on uncertain thought introduced the idea that it's not so much the exact values that matter, but more the way that they show roughly how a piece of evidence supports or denies a conclusion. In the last section we saw that it was better not to use probability methods in estimating the certainty of a conclusion. In fact, once you start working with beliefs and evidence there is nothing to say that you have to use probability at all! An alternative system is provided by fuzzy logic which is easiest to explain from the point of view of adjectives. If you think about the word 'tall' and how you use it you will realise that there is an element of uncertainty in how you apply it. It's not that someone has a probability of being tall rather that they are more or less tall. A 7ft person is almost certainly tall but what about someone 6ft 6 inches or 6 foot or 5 foot 9 inches? 'Tall' is clearly not something that can be easily distinguished by a yes/no type decision; it's more vague than that. In traditional logic, we use one to mean true and zero to mean false and there are no values in between. In fuzzy logic, you can use 'truth values' between zero and one and once again zero means false and one means true and intermediate values indicate 'more or less true or false'. For example, the answer to the question 'is he tall?' might not be a clear-cut 1 or 0 (i.e. yes or no) but 0.8 or 0.5 or some such intermediate value.

This idea of using intermediate truth values seems a little strange at first but it doesn't take too long to get used to it. The fundamental logical operations AND, OR and NOT generalise quite easily to fuzzy truth values:

    A AND B becomes MIN(A,B)
    A OR B becomes MAX(A,B)
    NOT(A) becomes 1−A

Thinking and reasoning: expert systems

irrespective of whether A and B are good old Boolean truth values or fuzzy logic. In other words, even in traditional logic, A AND B is equivalent to MIN(A,B):

A	B	A AND B	MIN(A,B)
0	0	0	0
0	1	0	0
1	0	0	0
1	1	1	1

This means that we can work with fuzzy logic and if the truth values happen to be zero and one we are doing nothing new; obviously traditional logic must be a subset of any new sort of reasoning that we are planning to use. From these simple beginnings we can go on to develop the whole of logic but now using fuzzy truth values.

There are many aspects of traditional logic that do not translate directly into fuzzy logic. This means that you cannot just replace traditional logic by fuzzy logic in any given application and to date nobody has really managed to work it into an expert system in any really convincing way, but it's early days yet!

One of the exciting uses for fuzzy logic is the description of human ideas to a computer. For example, the adjective 'tall' that was giving us so much trouble earlier could be described by a graph showing the truth value for various heights. This description is just as easy to convey to a computer as to another human. As well as simple descriptions of words such as 'tall', fuzzy logic can be used to convey vague rules such as 'if the boiler is hot' THEN 'turn the heat down' or IF 'the boiler is very hot' THEN 'turn the heat down a lot'. The words 'hot' 'very hot' and 'a lot' are all difficult to describe to a computer unless you are aware of the idea of fuzzy logic. This is one idea that has led to actual applications, such as controlling a steam engine and a cement kiln! You may have noticed that we have now come full circle. Chapters Two and Three were concerned with the idea of the heuristic rule as opposed to the algorithm. Heuristics are vague rules that *tend* to give you a solution rather than *always* give you a solution. What better way of describing a heuristic than as a fuzzy rule!

The condition and the conclusion

Before leaving the subject of reasoning using IF...THEN type rules it is worth showing how general the idea is. You might be surprised to discover that an expert system can be written to learn to play games of the sort described in Chapters Two and Three. This doesn't invalidate the theory of heuristics, move trees, evaluation functions and minimax strategy, rather it should be seen as consolidating them into a unified approach. The power of IF condition THEN conclusion comes from the vagueness of the terms 'condition' and 'conclusion'. The 'condition' could easily be a position in a game and the 'conclusion' the next move, instead of their being respectively a factual question and answer, as illustrated by Aardvark. The vagueness of the terms is also a major problem in implementing a more ambitious reasoning system. It is difficult to build into a program a mechanism for coping with the wide range of conditions and conclusions that human reasoning seems capable of working with. For the time being at least, it is up to the AI programmer to solve the problem of finding ways of representing conditions and implementing conclusions before the expert system can start to solve problems using its IF...THEN type rules.

Learning noughts and crosses

As already discussed noughts and crosses is a useful game to use to illustrate AI methods because it is easy enough to make the programs sufficiently short to be written in BASIC, while being difficult enough to make a good demonstration. So to illustrate the ideas involved in using an expert system to play games what better than to use noughts and crosses once again.

To be able to learn to do anything, the first requirement is a good memory. The reason for this is that to learn you must be able to remember what worked and what didn't. In the case of noughts and crosses you have to remember moves that lost you the game and then try to play them never again. A noughts and crosses board consists of nine playing positions each of which can either hold a blank, an X or a O. If we code blank as 0, the X as 1 and the O as 2 then any position in a game of noughts and crosses can be recorded as a sequence of digits consisting of only 0, 1 or 2. For example, 0000000010 would correspond to a board with eight blank positions and one X. It would be quite possible to record board positions by saving the digits as strings but in an effort to produce a program that will work on a wide variety of machines it is better to save the digits as numbers in an array. This method will only work with versions of BASIC that can store nine digit numbers. To find out if your version of BASIC can do this try

```
10 A=333333333
20 PRINT A
```

If the result printed is exactly the same as the number stored in A by line 10 then your BASIC can work with nine digit numbers. If this is

Thinking and reasoning: expert systems

not the case then you can either try to make use of integer variables (if your BASIC has these) or you can re-write the program to use strings.

The program given below uses the idea of saving board positions as nine digit numbers in the array M. Subroutine 5000 will convert the current position held in the two-dimensional array B into a single number stored in P. The program begins by offering the human player a move (subroutine 3000) and then recording in the array M the resulting board position. This is carried out by subroutine 4000, which calls subroutine 5000 to code the board position into a single number P, then checks to see if the board position is already stored in M using subroutine 6000 and, if it isn't, calls subroutine 6500 to store it.

So far we have a program that remembers new board positions as a game is played. But how does it choose its own move and how does it learn? The next stage in developing the program is to realise that the response to the human player's move simply depends on the current state of the board. This means that it is possible to think of playing noughts and crosses as

IF current position is X THEN make move Y

In other words, this is where the IF...THEN rules of the expert system come into play! Along with the array M there is a corresponding array R which is used to store responses. The way that this works is that if the current board position is stored in M(I) then the response is stored in R(I). The best way to store the response is using the same code as for the current board position. As the program hasn't learned anything about noughts and crosses as yet its response might as well be to the first free board location. This is indeed what happens. As each new board position is encountered subroutine 4000 saves it in M and in R and then calls subroutine 8000 to make a move into the first free space.

Obviously, almost random play of this sort is easy to beat and so the program remembers the details of each board position and what it played as a response but always loses! The next stage is to weed out bad IF...THEN rules. This is surprisingly easy to do. Let's suppose that the program has just lost a game then the move that it made just before it lost was a very bad move. The obvious thing to do is to search through memory to find the IF...THEN rule that lost the game and while leaving the IF... part alone change the response to the current board position that follows the THEN. As moves are made into the first free space, and this is marked in the nine digit number stored in R by 0, all we have to do to stop this being the response is to store a digit other than zero, 3 say, in this position. This is what subroutine 7500 does. Next time that the losing board position appears the program will play a different move as a response and if this once again loses the game it too will be 'blanked out' with a 3. This process of changing the move will continue until the correct, i.e. non-losing, response is found.

If you try running the program given below you will find that it is very easy to beat at first but slowly it learns how not to lose. And in noughts and crosses knowing how not to lose is almost as good as knowing how to win!

```
10 REM LEARNING TO PLAY
20 REM NOUGHTS AND CROSSES
30 GOSUB 1000
40 L=0:M=0
50 GOSUB 2000
55 M=M+1
60 GOSUB 3000
65 GOSUB 2000
66 GOSUB 8500
70 IF L<>0 THEN GOTO 9000
80 GOSUB 4000
85 GOSUB 2000
90 GOSUB 8500
95 M=M+1
100 IF L<>0 THEN GOTO 9000
110 GOTO 60

1000 DIM M(100),R(100)
1010 DIM B(3,3)
1020 N=100
1030 RETURN

2000 FOR I=1 TO 3
2010 FOR J=1 TO 3
2020 IF B(I,J)=0 THEN PRINT ".";
2030 IF B(I,J)=1 THEN PRINT "X";
2040 IF B(I,J)=2 THEN PRINT "O";
2060 NEXT J
2070 PRINT
2080 NEXT I
2090 RETURN

3000 PRINT
3010 PRINT "YOUR MOVE (ROW,COL)";
3020 INPUT R,C
3030 IF R>3 OR R<1 THEN GOTO 3010
3040 IF C>3 OR C<1 THEN GOTO 3010
3050 IF B(R,C)=0 THEN GOTO 3080
3060 PRINT "ALREADY OCCUPIED !"
3070 GOTO 3010
3080 B(R,C)=1
3090 RETURN
```

Thinking and reasoning: expert systems

```
4000 PRINT
4005 GOSUB 5000
4010 GOSUB 6000
4030 IF S>N THEN GOTO 4500
4040 IF F=0 THEN GOSUB 6500
4050 IF F=1 THEN GOSUB 7000
4060 RETURN

4500 PRINT "I HAVE RUN OUT OF MEMORY
4510 STOP

5000 P=0
5010 FOR I=1 TO 3
5020 FOR J=1 TO 3
5030 P=P*10+B(I,J)
5040 NEXT J
5050 NEXT I
5060 RETURN

6000 S=1
6010 F=0
6020 IF S>N THEN RETURN
6030 IF M(S)=0 THEN RETURN
6040 IF M(S)=P THEN F=1:RETURN
6050 S=S+1
6060 GOTO 6020

6500 M(S)=P
6510 Q=P
6520 R(S)=P
6530 GOSUB 8000
6540 RETURN

7000 Q=R(S)
7010 GOSUB 8000
7020 RETURN

7500 Q=R(S)
7510 X=0:Y=0
7520 A=Q-INT(Q/10)*10
7530 Q=INT(Q/10)
7540 X=X+1
7550 IF A<>0 THEN GOTO 7520
7560 Y=4
7570 IF X=1 THEN GOTO 7610
7580 FOR I=1 TO X-1
7590 Y=Y*10
7600 NEXT I
7610 R(S)=R(S)+Y
7620 RETURN

8000 X=0
8010 A=Q-INT(Q/10)*10
8020 Q=INT(Q/10)
```

```
8030 X=X+1
8040 IF A=0 THEN GOTO 8100
8050 IF X=9 THEN L=1:RETURN
8060 GOTO 8010

8100 X=9-X
8110 R=INT(X/3)
8120 C=X-R*3
8130 B(R+1,C+1)=2
8140 RETURN

8500 FOR I=1 TO 3
8510 IF B(I,1)=1 AND B(I,2)=1 AND B(I,3)=1
     THEN L=1
8520 IF B(I,1)=2 AND B(I,2)=2 AND B(I,3)=2
     THEN L=2
8530 IF B(1,I)=1 AND B(2,I)=1 AND B(3,I)=1
     THEN L=1
8540 IF B(1,I)=2 AND B(2,I)=2 AND B(3,I)=2
     THEN L=2
8550 NEXT I
8560 IF B(1,1)=1 AND B(2,2)=1 AND B(3,3)=1
     THEN L=1
8570 IF B(1,1)=2 AND B(2,2)=2 AND B(3,3)=2
     THEN L=2
8580 IF B(1,3)=1 AND B(2,2)=1 AND B(3,1)=1
     THEN L=1
8590 IF B(1,3)=2 AND B(2,2)=2 AND B(3,1)=2
     THEN L=2
8600 RETURN

9000 IF L<>1 THEN GOTO 9050
9010 PRINT "YOU WIN..."
9020 PRINT "BUT I WILL LEARN FROM MY MISTAKE!"
9040 GOSUB 7500
9050 IF M=9 THEN GOTO 9100
9060 PRINT "I WIN"
9100 PRINT "ANOTHER GAME ";
9110 INPUT A$
9120 IF LEFT$(A$,1)="N" THEN STOP
9130 FOR I=1 TO 3
9140 FOR J=1 TO 3
9150 B(I,J)=0
9160 NEXT J
9170 NEXT I
9180 GOTO 40
```

You should be able to work out the details of the program for yourself but to help the subroutine structure is

   10   main program
 1000   initialisation
 2000   print board
 3000   human's move

```
4000  computer's move (uses other subroutines)
5000  code board position into a single number
6000  find current position in M
6500  position not found, store in M and R
7000  position found get response from R
7500  lost game so remove first 0 in losing move
8000  find first free position for computer's move
8500  has anyone won yet?
9000  end of game
```

Aardvark and noughts and crosses

You should be able to see similarities and differences between the Aardvark program and the noughts and crosses expert system. Both programs make use of the IF 'condition' THEN 'conclusion' type rule but the 'conditions' and 'conclusions' in each case are different. In Aardvark's case, the 'condition' is a potentially long list of attributes connected together by AND but in the case of noughts and crosses the 'condition' is a particular board position represented as a digit code. However it is important not to allow the difference in representation obscure the fact that these conditions are of the same type. For example, the board position could be coded as 'an X in the top right hand corner AND an X in the bottom righthand corner AND...' and so once again they could be represented by a tree structure! The conclusion is more obviously different in each case. Aardvark's conclusions are decisions about animals and are either right or wrong but the noughts and crosses program generates moves which only prove to be right or wrong at a subsequent point in the game. The programs also learn in different ways. The Aardvark program has to ask a human how to avoid the mistake it has just made but the noughts and crosses program can delete the faulty rule from its set of all possible rules to avoid making the mistake again. The key difference between the two programs are that the Aardvark program cannot know in advance all the rules that might be used to distinguish animals but the noughts and crosses program can, and in fact does, make a list of all the possible move rules.

Nought and crosses and game playing

There is plenty of scope for improvement and further study in the noughts and crosses program. In particular, by comparing its approach to the game and the more traditional minimax approach you should be able to see ways in which other expert systems can be improved. For example, there is one game that it will never learn to avoid losing. This is the same game that the one-ply noughts and crosses program lost. Indeed if you analyse the program carefully you will find that the expert system is only looking one move ahead when it removes poor rules. The game tree is still with us! To increase the rule selection to the equivalent of a two-ply search isn't difficult. You simply have to ask yourself why the program will never learn to avoid losing that one particular game and what should be done about it.

The universal expert?

This chapter has tended to emphasise the usefulness of the expert or rule-based approach to AI. However it has to be admitted that it is difficult to believe that a game such as chess is played using a rule-based system of inference similar to the one used to play noughts and crosses. This is because even storing, let alone matching, all the board positions for chess is clearly impossible — there are far too many. It is possible that chess is played by a rule-based system but the conditions are not simply board positions; there must be some sort of overall heuristic coupled with a local analysis of the current state of play. The point is that the difficulty in applying rule-based systems to a wide range of AI problems may be finding a good representation of the conditions and the conclusions.

You may also feel that expert systems are missing the fundamental human ability to invent and investigate new rules. That is, expert systems lack the part of thinking that loosely corresponds to creativity. This is true and most expert systems have to obtain their rules from an existing human expert. However, one or two experimental programs are able not only to process their rules to obtain new and simpler rules, they can also deduce completely new rules by examining the input information. You could try to improve Aardvark to remove redundant rules and speculate on the existence of new rules but this is not easy!

5

The structure of memory

A large part of every computer is concerned with storing data. However, computer memory and human memory are very different. Information that is stored in the brain is accessible in a way that information in a computer is not. Currently computer memory is used more like an electronic equivalent of a book than the brain.

If you need a piece of information held in a computer then you have to know exactly where it is stored. For example, if you want to find out the telephone number of someone and you know the name then you can use a computer data base in the same way that you use a telephone directory. However, if you know various things about the person, but not his name, then the computer data base is a useless as a telephone directory. Even if you have a photograph of the person and a complete life history the only thing that will ensure the retrieval of his telephone number from a computer data base is his name. Compare this to the many ways in which the same information can be retrieved from the human memory. A photograph, a description or just a fragment of the name is often enough to recall a telephone number. The difference seems to stem from the way that human memory is much more closely connected with the processing of the information than the computer's memory.

The nature of human memory

It is clear that human memory is not a simple mechanism. Indeed it is most likely not even a single mechanism! Psychologists have traditionally identified two sorts of memory – long term and short term. However, the more recent view is that memory isn't really organised into these two neat categories and is in fact a collection of a diverse set of memory functions. It is also clear that memory itself is not entirely separate from the processes of reasoning and thinking. In other words, our identification of a memory component of human thought may be more of a convenience rather than having any correspondence to a real division. While this may be so, there is still much of practical value to be learned by studying memory in isolation from thinking.

A moment's introspection will confirm that there is a memory function associated with each of our senses. Although they are not all equally developed, we can remember images, sounds, touch, taste and smell. In addition to these sense-oriented memories, there is also a sort of general memory facility that seems to be directly involved in reasoning. This general memory constitutes an internal 'model of the world' that enables us to recall objects, their properties and their relationships with one another. It is this more general form of memory and the way that it interacts with language that is of the most practical interest to AI.

This general memory is by its very nature 'long term', and indeed short-term memory is a much simpler form of storage. The best example of short-term memory is trying to remember a telephone number that you have just been told. In general, it is an isolated collection of digits that you can remember accurately for a short time only. This sort of memory can be accounted for by supposing that the digit sequence is kept in storage by 'recycling' it. Recycling avoids the storage problem by never letting the data come to rest! For example, in early computers mercury delay lines were used as recycling stores. (See Figure 5.1) The data was stored as a stream of acoustic pulses that propagated through the mercury until they were picked up by a microphone at one end, amplified and then re-injected back into the tube by a speaker at the other end. In the mercury delay line, you can clearly see that the data is stored by being kept on the move.

In human short-term memory, you can sometimes see the same effect when someone rehearses a telephone number (by repeatedly saying it out loud) to improve their chances of remembering it. The physical mechanisms of short-term memory could easily be based on electrical activity in the brain 'echoing' around loops made up of neurons (see Chapter Eight). A fact that tends to support the loop theory of short-term memory is that it seems to be limited on average to storing seven different pieces of information. This fixed size limitation may correspond to the physical capacity of the loop.

In practice, things are likely to be much more complicated than this, but whatever the exact mechanism of short-term memory it is not as important to AI as long-term memory because we already have good mechanical substitutes that can play the role of short-term memory — a note pad or a computer!

If information is kept in short-term memory for long enough it will be transferred to long-term memory. The mechanism of long-term memory is far more complicated and it is far from clear whether it is the result of physical or chemical changes in the brain. Once in long-term memory information forms 'links' with other existing pieces of information and these links are as much the essential

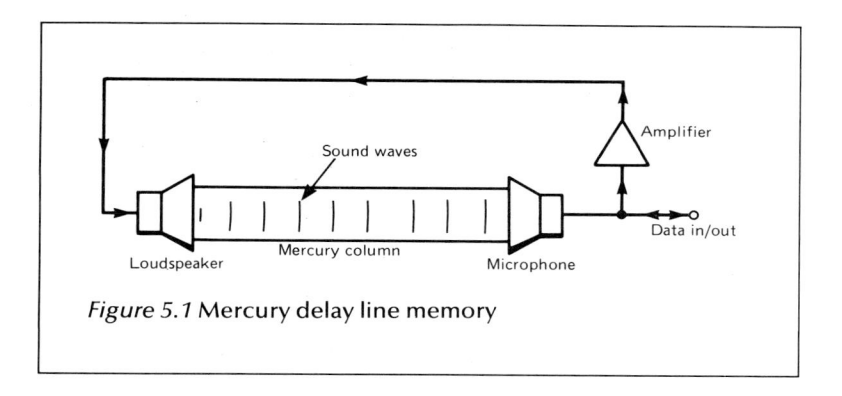

Figure 5.1 Mercury delay line memory

difference between short and long-term memory as the length of time that they work for! To demonstrate the number of links that any piece of information has with others, all you have to do is to think of one thing and then write down everything else that 'comes to mind'. Long-term memory is more like a network of information than a simple note pad.

The nature of computer memory

Most computers separate the processing and memory functions into quite distinct units — the CPU and RAM. These units interact in very restricted ways compared with human thought and memory. For example, a computer memory will store a piece of information without change and it will recall exactly what is required and no more. Indeed a computer memory that retrieved more than was desired or changed data in any way would be sent to a workshop for repair! In this sense, computer memory is entirely 'passive' and plays about as much part in processing as pencil and paper play in arithmetic.

Computer memory is further restricted by only being able to store numbers of fixed size. However, this restriction is more a characteristic of the technology used to implement the memory than of the principle of operation. The most important feature of computer memory is that it is an 'addressable store'. Each item of information in store is paired with another item of information called its 'address'. Information is recalled from such a memory by supplying its address (See Figure 5.2). In this sense, an addressable store works by pairing up two items of information:

```
item 1   |   item 2
address  |   data
```

Normally the form of the first item of data, the address, is simple and regular. For example, a computer memory is an addressable store that uses a limited range of numbers as addresses. The use of

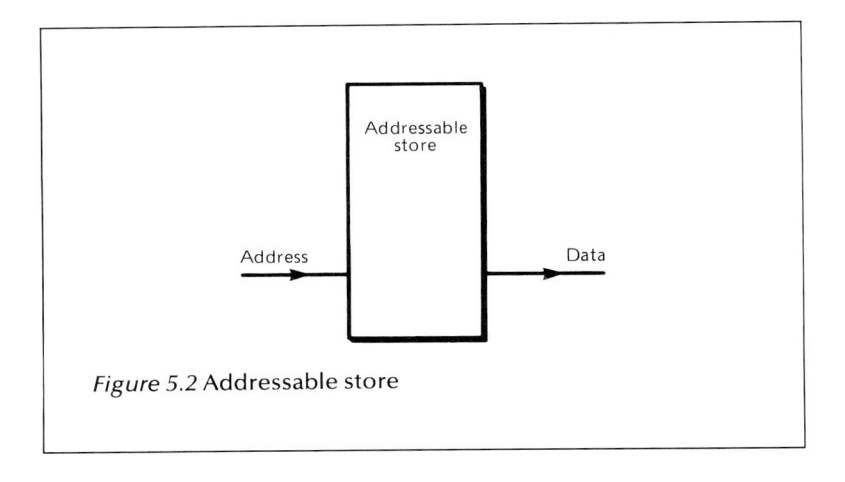

Figure 5.2 Addressable store

numeric addresses is so common that there is a tendency to think that all addresses are numeric. However, this is far from the truth. A typical use of an addressable store would be to remember a list of telephone numbers using the surname of the person owning the telephone as the address. This addressable store could be implemented in many different technologies, e.g. paper technology gives a standard telephone directory!

To summarise: the principle that lies behind computer memory and other types of addressable store is the pairing of two pieces of information, the address and the data. The address is associated with the data as it is stored and it is used to request the recall of the data from the store. To ensure that each item of data is identified, each address must be unique.

The recall problem: associative memory

If you are familiar with the workings of computer memory then, apart from the widening of the address to include any sort of data, you will find nothing strange in the above description of an addressable store. The fact that computer memory works is useful and is clearly an associative store tends to cover up the problem inherent in all associative stores. However, if you are not familiar with computer memory, you might have detected the nature of the problem in the similarity of the description of the data and the address. The trouble is to recall anything from an addressable store you must have its address and, as the both the address and the data can be the same type of information, why should you be any more likely to be in possession of the address than the data? In practice the only time an addressable store is of any use at all is when the addresses are either simple or form a simple system. For example, the only reason that a telephone directory is useful is that names tend to be easier to remember than telephone numbers. In general, the address is a smaller 'quantity' of information that can be used as a sort of 'handle' for a much larger quantity of information. For example, in *Who's Who* a person's name is used as an address for the, perhaps, hundreds of words describing them!

The use of an address to recall data is both the strength and the weakness of an addressable store. For applications for which the use of a single address works, there is nothing more efficient than an addressable store. However, many applications do not fit into this very simple scheme. For example, consider the apparently easy task of finding the name corresponding to a telephone number. If the information has been stored using name as the address and telephone number as the data the problem is a lot more difficult. Using a conventional addressable store the only solution is to examine the data associated with each address in turn until the desired telephone number is found. The point is that an addressable store will retrieve data corresponding to a given address and what this problem requires is a store that will retrieve the address given the data! You may be thinking that the solution is to simply use the telephone number as the address and the name as data. The trouble with this suggestion is that there can be more than one name per telephone number and this would violate the requirement of a unique address for each item of data. The real trouble with an addressable store is the address determines the data directly but not vice versa (see Figure 5.3). To a certain extent this arrangement misses the essential similarity between address and data. You could say that the only thing that marks out the address is the fact that you know it and want to know the data that it is associated with.

Memories that will retrieve addresses that are paired with an item of data are available and are called associative memories, also referred to as Content Addressable Memory (CAM) (see Figure 5.4). Notice that an associative memory will retrieve all of the addresses paired with a given item of data. Associative stores are very useful and as they can be easily implemented in hardware they offer the prospect of faster computers. In the future you can expect to see

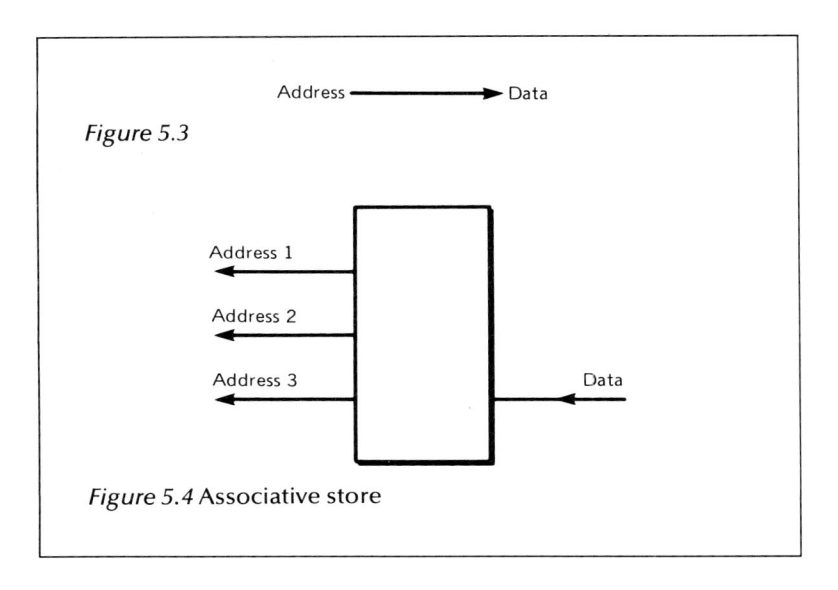

Figure 5.3

Address ⟶ Data

Figure 5.4 Associative store

Address 1 ⟵
Address 2 ⟵
Address 3 ⟵
Data ⟵

machines with both types of memory, addressable store and associative memory. However, neither type of memory really begins to tackle the true deficiencies of the simple pairing of an address with data.

Relational stores

A memory has to not only store information, it has to form links or relationships between items of information. The sophistication of the memory depends not so much on raw storage capacity but on the variety of relationships that it can maintain. The simplest sort of memory that we have looked at so far, computer memory, forms links between pairs of items as shown in Figure 5.5. The notion of one item of information being the address and the other the data is entirely due to the rules governing the way the links are made. The

The structure of memory

most sophisticated memory that we have looked at, the human memory, is characterised by the wide variety of links that are made between items of information stored within it. Indeed the links can be made in such a free way that the ideas of address and data have to be modified. That is an item of information may be used to recall another, which is then used to recall yet another and so on. An item of information is an address when it is known and being used to recall other items of information associated with it.

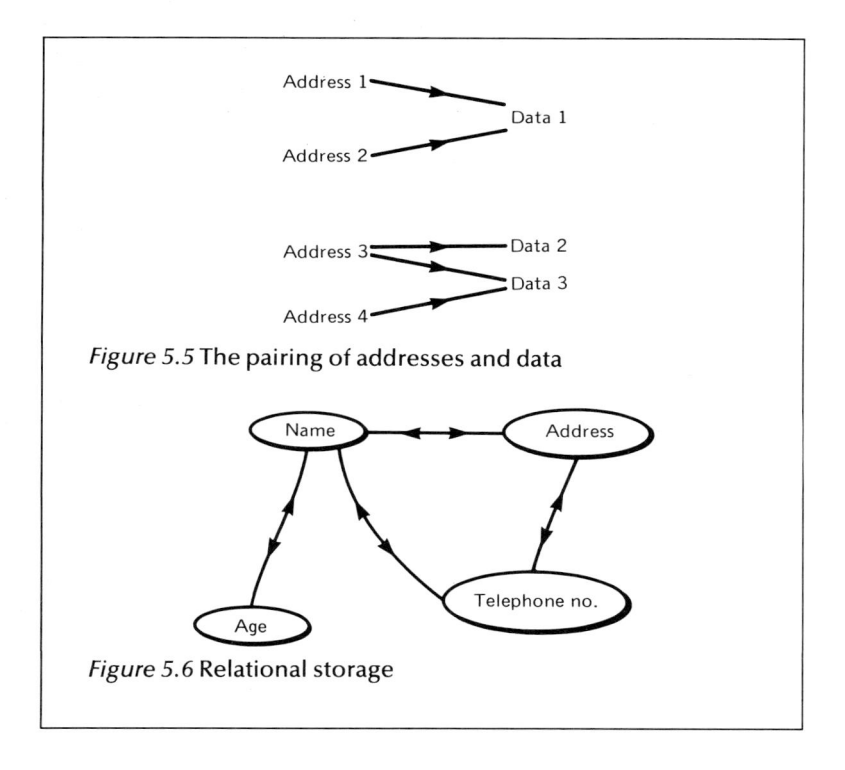

Figure 5.5 The pairing of addresses and data

Figure 5.6 Relational storage

This suggests that if we want to construct more sophisticated memories it is worth investigating methods of increasing the ways of linking items of information together. The first and most obvious improvement is to allow any number of links in any direction to exist between any pair of items. This scheme gives rise to a relational store. For example, in Figure 5.6 separate items of information are linked together so that for example, 'name' can be found from 'address' or 'telephone' number and vice versa. Notice that relational store can give results that you might not expect. For example, if (using the structure of Figure 5.6) you use 'name' as an address to find 'age' then you will recall one piece of information, i.e. the age of the person but if you use 'age' as an address you will get a list of all the people of a particular age. The relational store doesn't make hard and fast distinctions between addresses and data but you cannot expect all of its links to work in the same way.

A modified but practical form of the relational store lies at the heart of a wide range of commercial software, usually called 'relational data bases'. A relational data base holds lists of information and uses 'pointers' to enable information to be stored economically and recalled using a variety of addresses. Relational data bases have the potential to become an important part of AI research in the next few years. However, the relational data base is not the final word in increased sophistication.

Conceptual stores

The links that we have been using to associate one item of data with another have so far all been of the same type. They are anonymous arrows or pointers that simply bind items of information together without indicating what it is that causes them to be joined. A human memory is very different because it links items together with named relationships. For example, in Figure 5.7 the relationships between

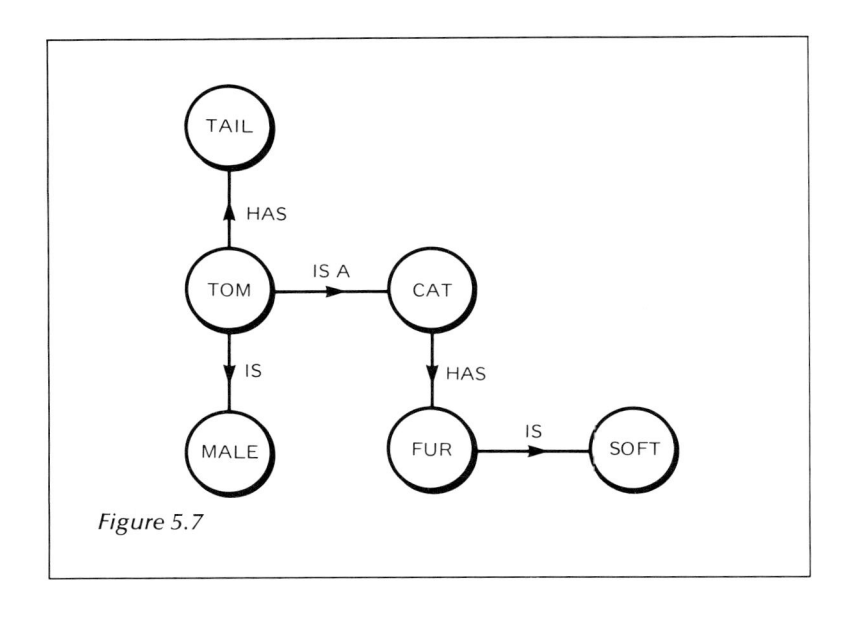

Figure 5.7

The structure of memory 73

the items of information TOM, CAT, TAIL, FUR, SOFT and MALE are shown. You can see that the relationship between TOM and CAT is different to that between TOM and TAIL, namely TOM *IS A* CAT but TOM *HAS* FUR. The fact that the relationships *IS A* and *HAS* are different only really becomes apparent when the memory is being searched. For example, if you want the question DOES TOM HAVE FUR answered then as well as looking at the item TOM for *HAS* relations you have to also examine the items connected to TOM by *IS A* relations. Thus the answer to DOES TOM HAVE FUR is found by examining the *HAS* relationships coming from CAT, i.e.,

TOM→IS A→CAT→HAS→FUR

means that TOM does have fur.

The named relationship between two items of information can be called a 'concept' and so the sort of memory that we are discussing is called a 'conceptual store'. In general, a conceptual store can be very complicated but it is possible to produce a small example in BASIC to show how things work and to provide the starting point for experiments.

A general conceptual data base program

To produce a program that will store a system of items and named relationships, it is first necessary to solve the problem of representing the named links. Each item of information can be stored in an element of a string array W$, say. When an item is encountered it is simply stored in the next free element of the array. The item that it is linked to is of course also stored in the array and we could indicate which one it was by storing its index in another array P. For example, if the array W$ contained

W$(1) = "TOM"
W$(2) = "TAIL"
W$(3) = "CAT"
W$(4) = "FUR"

Then the link between TOM and TAIL and CAT and FUR would be stored in P as

P(1) = 2
P(2) = 0
P(3) = 4
P(4) = 0

In other words, the item that W$(I) is linked to is stored in P(I). A value of P(I) of zero indicates that the item is not linked to anything.

This combined use of arrays W$ and P gives us a simple relational data base because, although the links are all represented, they are anonymous. The simplest way of storing the names of the links is as items of information in the array W$! To associate the name of the link with its use we also have to use another array R to store the index of the name. So

W$(I) is an item
P(I)   is the index of the item it
       is linked to, i.e. it is linked
       to W$(P(I))
R(I)   is the index of the name of the
       relationship, i.e. W$(R(I)) is
       the name of the relationship

For example, adding the names of the relationships to the previous contents of W$ gives

W$(1) = "TOM": P(1) = 2: R(1) = 5
W$(2) = "TAIL": P(2) = 2: R(2) = 0
W$(3) = "CAT": P(3) = 2: R(3) = 6
W$(4) = "FUR": P(4) = 2: R(4) = 0
W$(5) = "HAS": P(5) = 2: R(5) = 0
W$(6) = "IS A": P(6) = 2: R(6) = 0

Thus W$(1), TOM, is related to W$(P(1)), TAIL, and the relationship is W$(R(1)), *HAS*. Notice that the value of R(1) is set to zero when there is no relationship to label.

The only remaining problem is what happens when there is more than one link from an item. This could be dealt with by making both P and R two-dimensional arrays and using them to store all the links and the names of the realtionships for each item. So, P(1,1) would store the first link for the first item and P(1,2) would store the second link for the first item and so on. The solution adopted by the program given below is simpler but can be slower. Each time an item appears it is stored in the array W$, even if it is already present in the array. So to add TOM IS MALE to the memory the three items TOM, IS and MALE are stored in W$, and P and R are set to point to the correct items, i.e.,

W$(7) = "TOM": P(7) = 8: R(7) = 9
W$(8) = "MALE": P(8) = 0: R(8) = 0
W$(9) = "IS A": P(9) = 0: R(9) = 0

In practice this duplication of items allows us to store information in the memory without checking to see if it is already there and doesn't cause any practical problems.

The structure of memory

Now that the problem of representing the structure of a conceptual store has been solved all that is left is to work out how information gets into it and how information can be retrieved. The simplest way of allowing the user to store information is via the English sentence construction.

x relation y

were x and y are items to be stored and connected by the link named 'relation' for example,

```
TOM IS A CAT
TOM IS MALE
TOM HAS TAIL
CAT HAS FUR
FUR IS SOFT
```

describe the information shown in Figure 5.7. Using this limited form of English ensures that it is possible for the program to separate x and y from the relation. The rule used is that the first word is item x, the last word is item y and any words in between form a description of the relationship.

Once information has been entered the memory is only useful if it can be used to answer questions about its contents. Using the form of representation that has been described it is possible to implement many different types of question-answering routines but, to keep things simple, the program given below only attempts to handle the following three types of question:

```
TELL ME ABOUT x
DOES x HAVE y
IS x A y
```

Once again because of the restricted format of these questions it is easy for the program to detect the type of the question and the items mentioned within it. The first question is detected by the first word being TELL and the last word is taken to be x, similarly the second and third questions are detected by the first word being DOES or IS respectively and the second word is taken to be x and the last word is taken to be y.

What happens when one of the three questions is detected varies according to the question? To answer the TELL ME ABOUT x question the program has to search for all occurrences of x in W$ and then print out the relationship W$(R(I)) and the item it is related to W$(P(I)). However, if this is all it did the question TELL ME ABOUT TOM would have the answer TOM IS A CAT – HAS TAIL – IS MALE. By following the IS A relationship to CAT you can also discover that TOM HAS FUR — IS SOFT. To answer the question completely, the program should follow all of the relationships out of TOM through all of the memory. So the programs response to TELL ME ABOUT x is to print every connection that x has with everything else in the memory! To answer the DOES x HAVE y question, it is necessary to not only examine the direct HAS relationships but the HAS relationships of items connected to x by IS A relationships. So DOES TOM HAVE FUR would be answered by the following chain of relationships:

TOM→IS A→CAT→HAS→FUR

Similarly the IS x A y question has to be answered by following IS A relationships. So if we add CAT IS A ANIMAL to the memory the answer to the question IS TOM A ANIMAL would be answered by the following chain of relationships:

TOM→IS A→CAT→IS A→ANIMAL

The need to examine not only direct relationships but follow chains of relationships of a specific kind is in general difficult to implement without using advanced techniques, specifically recursion. The simplest way of following such chains in BASIC is to use a stack to store all the intermediate findings. A stack is simply a temporary store that is used via two operations PUSH and PULL. PUSH will store an item of information and PULL will retrieve it. The order that information is retrieved is opposite to the order that it was stored, i.e. the last item to be PUSHed is the first item to be retrieved by a PULL. For this application the order that items are retrieved is not important, the stack is simply used as a temporary store for relevant links that have still to be explored.

The way that this works is best illustrated by an example of how the DOES x HAVE y question is handled with reference to the data in Figure 5.7. The question DOES TOM HAVE FUR is answered by first scanning W$ for the word TOM. When the word is found the type of the relationship is checked. If it is HAS y then the item y has to be checked to see if is FUR. If it is, then the question is answered. If it is not, then the array is searched or another occurrence of TOM. However, if an IS A y relationship is found then the index of the item y is PUSHed on the stack. Once the whole of W$ has been searched for all occurrences of TOM then the search has to be repeated with any items that are stored on the stack until the stack is empty.

In the case of the information in Figure 5.7, the first occurrence of TOM is a HAS relationship but this does not answer the question. The TOM IS entry cannot provide any information regarding the

The structure of memory

question and so it is ignored but the TOM IS A entry results in the pointer to CAT being PUSHed onto the stack. At the end of the first scan through the array the question is not answered but there is something on the stack that still has to be explored. The information on the stack is retrieved and then the array W$ is searched for ocurrence of CAT HAS and CAT IS A relationships. Fortunately in this case the first CAT HAS entry answers the question and no further searching is required. However, in principle any IS A relationships detected on the second search would be PUSHed onto the stack, so causing W$ to be searched yet again. You should be able to see that all that is happening is that the stack is being used as a temporary store for further items that have to be searched for HAS relationships that might answer the question or IS A relationships that extend the search.

Putting all this together results in the following program

```
  10 GOSUB 1000
  20 INPUT A$
  30 T$=A$
  40 GOSUB 2000
  50 IF K$="TELL" THEN GOSUB 3000:GOTO 20
  60 IF K$="DOES" THEN GOSUB 4000:GOTO 20
  70 IF K$="IS" THEN GOSUB 5000:GOTO 20
  80 X$=K$
  90 GOSUB 6000
 100 GOSUB 7000
 110 GOTO 20

1000 N=50
1010 DIM W$(N)
1020 DIM T(N)
1030 DIM R(N)
1040 DIM P(N)
1050 R=0
1060 DIM M(N)
1070 T=1
1080 RETURN

2000 K$=""
2010 IF LEN(T$)=0 THEN RETURN
2015 IF LEFT$(T$,1)<>" " THEN GOTO 2040
2020 T$=RIGHT$(T$,LEN(T$)-1)
2030 GOTO 2010
2040 K$=K$+LEFT$(T$,1)
2050 T$=RIGHT$(T$,LEN(T$)-1)
2060 IF LEFT$(T$,1)=" " THEN GOTO 2080
2070 GOTO 2040
```

```
2080 IF LEN(T$)=0 THEN RETURN
2090 T$=RIGHT$(T$,LEN(T$)-1)
2100 IF LEFT$(T$,1)<>" " THEN RETURN
2110 GOTO 2080

3000 X$=""
3010 GOSUB 2000
3020 IF LEN(T$)=0 THEN GOTO 3040
3030 GOTO 3010
3040 X$=K$
3045 F=0
3050 FOR I=1 TO S
3060 IF W$(I)<>X$ THEN GOTO 3110
3064 IF P(I)=0 THEN GOTO 3110
3065 F=F+1
3070 IF F=1 THEN PRINT X$;" ";
3080 PRINT W$(R(I));" ";
3090 PRINT W$(P(I))
3095 D=P(I)
3100 GOSUB 8000
3110 NEXT I
3120 IF F=0 THEN GOTO 3200
3130 IF T=1 THEN RETURN
3140 GOSUB 8100
3150 X$=W$(D)
3160 GOTO 3050
3200 PRINT "I DON'T KNOW ANYTHING ABOUT ";X$
3210 PRINT "PERHAPS YOU WOULD LIKE TO TELL
     ME ABOUT ";X$
3220 RETURN

4000 GOSUB 2000
4010 X$=K$
4020 IF LEN(T$)=0 THEN GOTO 4050
4030 GOSUB 2000
4040 GOTO 4020
4050 Y$=K$
4055 K$=X$
4060 F=0:A=0
4070 FOR I=1 TO S
4080 IF W$(I)<>X$ THEN GOTO 4110
4085 F=1
4090 IF W$(R(I))=" IS A" THEN D=P(I):GOSUB 8000
4100 IF W$(R(I))=" HAS A" THEN D=P(I):GOSUB 8000:
     GOSUB 8200
4105 IF W$(R(I))=" HAS" THEN D=P(I):GOSUB 8000:
     GOSUB 8200
4110 NEXT I
4120 IF T=1 THEN GOTO  4170
4130 GOSUB 8100
4140 IF D=0 THEN GOTO 4120
4150 X$=W$(D)
4160 GOTO 4070
4170 IF F=0 THEN PRINT "NO INFORMATION ON ";K$
```

The structure of memory

```
4180 IF F=1 AND A=0 THEN PRINT "NOT AS FAR AS
     I KNOW"
4190 IF F=1 AND A=1 THEN PRINT "YES"
4200 RETURN

5000 GOSUB 2000
5005 X$=K$
5010 GOSUB 2000
5020 IF LEN(T$)<>0 THEN GOTO 5010
5030 Y$=K$
5040 K$=X$
5050 F=0:A=0
5060 FOR I=1 TO S
5070 IF W$(I)<>X$ THEN GOTO 5100
5080 F=1
5090 IF W$(R(I))=" IS A" THEN D=P(I):GOSUB 8000:
     GOSUB 8200
5100 NEXT I
5110 IF T=1 THEN GOTO 4170
5120 GOSUB 8100
5130 IF D<>0 THEN X$=W$(D):GOTO 5060
5140 GOTO 5110

6000 R$=""
6010 GOSUB 2000
6020 IF LEN(T$)=0 THEN GOTO 6050
6030 R$=R$+" "+K$
6040 GOTO 6010
6050 Y$=K$
6060 RETURN

7000 S=S+1
7010 W$(S)=X$
7020 T(S)=4
7030 W$(S+1)=R$
7040 T(S+1)=2
7050 W$(S+2)=Y$
7060 R(S)=S+1
7070 P(S)=S+2
7080 S=S+2
7090 RETURN

8000 IF T>N THEN RETURN
8010 M(T)=D
8020 T=T+1
8030 RETURN

8100 IF T=1 THEN RETURN
8110 T=T-1
8120 D=M(T)
8130 RETURN

8200 IF W$(P(I))=Y$ THEN A=1
8210 RETURN
```

To help you understand the program the subroutine structure is

      10   Main program
           Input data and decide if it is question or new data
    1000   Initialisation
    2000   Remove the next word in T$ and store it in K$
    3000   TELL subroutine
    4000   DOES subroutine
    5000   IS subroutine
    6000   Add information to W$
    8000   Push number in D on stack
    8100   Pull number from stack and store in D
    8200   Compare W$(P(I)) with Y$ and set A to 1 if they are equal

Using the conceptual data base

The program given above implements only a few of the ideas of a conceptual data base and yet it still behaves in an interesting way, as the output given below indicates. For clarity, all the input data and questions are shown in upper case and the computer's responses are in lower case.

    TOM HAS A TAIL
    TOM IS MALE
    TOM IS A CAT
    CAT HAS FUR
    FUR IS SOFT
    IS TOM A CAT
    yes
    DOES TOM HAVE A TAIL
    yes
    TAIL HAS STRIPES
    CAT IS A ANIMAL
    IS TOM A ANIMAL
    yes
    DOES TOM HAVE STRIPES
    yes
    DOES CAT HAVE STRIPES
    not as far as I know

There is a great deal more that can be done to improve this program. At the simple level of implementation, the method that it uses to store the names of relationships is very inefficient. The program should occasionally scan through the array W$ and remove multiple occurrences of the name of any relationships and adjust any relationship pointers in R(I) to point at the single occurrence of each relationship. At a more sophisticated level, it should be possible to recognise different categories or classes of objects in the store. For example, TOM is an unique object but CAT is a class to which other objects can belong. Such classes can be detected because of the following IS A relationships. In fact, the program already includes the array T, which records the type of each item as accurately as it is known when it is entered, although this type information isn't used.

T(I) = 1 means the item is an object
T(I) = 2 means the item is a relationship
T(I) = 3 means the item is a class
T(I) = 4 means the item is either a class or an object.

You can also introduce new relationships and include them in question processing. For example, TOM IS A CAT implies that TOM has all the items that CAT has but the reverse is not true. In fact the new relationship that is necessary is

CAT EXAMPLE IS TOM

Given this relationship, any items that TOM HAS might also be items that CAT HAS. In this way, you could arrange for the answer to DOES CAT HAVE STRIPES to be AT LEAST SOMETIMES. If other examples of CAT also turned out to have stripes then you might feel justified to conclude that CAT HAS STRIPES.

By experimenting with the above program, you will discover many ways of examining and reorganising the relationships between the items. There is one danger to be aware of while using the program, namely circular relationships. A relationship of the form TOM IS A CAT and CAT IS A TOM will send the program into an infinite loop! The danger is not so much that you will enter such obviously circular definitions but that they will be built up as a long chain of IS A relationships.

Remembering to think

The way that conceptual memory is involved in thinking, as well as just storing, information should be obvious from the above examples. The type of relationship that exists between two items governs what sort of reasoning can be applied. What is interesting about the program given in this chapter is that it stores the type of the relationship in exactly the same way that it stores other items. This means, in principle at least, that it is possible to enter relationships between relationships! The connection between reasoning and memory has yet to be exploited in any convincing way. This suggests that there is a lot of work to be done in finding ways of combining conceptual memory with expert systems!

6

Pattern recognition

It is sometimes difficult to see any overall themes in artificial intelligence. Some ideas, such as trees, crop up in a wide range of applications but it is often difficult to see why. This is a reflection of the fact that, at the moment at least, there is no overall theory of AI. There are, however, a number of areas of AI that have managed to produce such general theories that they can claim to be contenders for the title of *the* theory of AI. 'Pattern Recognition' is one such area.

Although pattern recognition started off as a study of artificial vision, and hence the term 'pattern' implied a visual pattern, the term is easily extended to include such things as patterns of sound and patterns of events of all kinds. For example, the problem of playing two-person games, such as chess or noughts and crosses, could be thought of in terms of recognising patterns of moves and pieces. From this point of view, it is not difficult to see why pattern recognition can begin to give a total view of AI. In truth, the situation is not so clear cut. Most areas of AI use pattern recognition techniques somewhere but usually in combination with other methods and theories that tend to be just as important. If you feel, however, that a subject called 'pattern recognition' is too specialised to be of interest to you then you are wrong! The activity of recognising or detecting a 'pattern' is far too general an aspect of intelligent behaviour to be ignored. In terms of the IF 'condition' THEN 'conclusion' rules that were described in Chapter Four, it could be said that pattern recognition is concerned with the complicated problem of implementing the 'condition' part of the rule.

Recognition and learning

Humans are the best general-purpose recognisers that we can study. Although they can often be out-performed at a specific task, so far there is nothing so versatile as a human. In fact, as mentioned elsewhere in this book, humans are sometimes a little too good at recognising patterns, tending to see something where nothing exists. Most approaches to artificial pattern recognition are attempts to copy the way humans recognise things. However, there are two distinct ways of going about this. You can either ignore the fact that humans *learn* to recognise things or make it fundamental to your method. A newly-born human recognises very little indeed. After repeated exposure to patterns, the number of things recognised increases rapidly. Even after many other mental abilities are fully developed the mature human still continues to learn to recognise new patterns. If you were sufficiently keen, it would be quite possible for you to learn to recognise the words of a foreign language and even a new written alphabet. Indeed, we all expect to be able to recognise a new face after only one or possibly two meetings and would be as upset as the owner of the face if this ability failed! The fact that humans learn to recognise patterns has resulted in a general approach to pattern recognition that involves 'training' a program or even a machine to recognise patterns. This has caused a great deal of the study of learning to be submerged in pattern recognition. The alternative approach is to say that the learning is an incidental part of pattern recognition and all we are interested in is the resulting recogniser rather than the way it came about.

For practical applications, it often seems better to try to build a machine or write a program that recognises whatever you are interested in rather than tackle the more general problem of a machine that learns to recognise a range of things. For example, if you wanted to recognise letters of the alphabet automatically (a problem that is dear to the Post Office's heart) then why not approach the problem by writing a program to recognise the letter A then the letter B and so on? The trouble is that you have to *know* how to recognise the letter A to be able to write a program to do it although you may be able to recognise a letter A you probably have a very vague idea about how you do it! If you take the apparently more difficult course and try to build a machine or write a program that will learn to recognise the alphabet then you needn't know anything about how you achieve the same result. All you have to do is to present examples of the letters of the alphabet and allow the machine to classify them. If it classifies an example correctly all is well. If it misclassifies an example, however, all the human has to do is to inform it of its error and what the correct classification is. In other words, rather than build-in knowledge of how humans classify letters of the alphabet, we can allow the program to learn by example; we can train it to recognise anything that we can.

As mentioned in Chapter One, these two approaches – the learning/developing approach and the direct solution approach –

can be seen in all areas of AI. They give rise to the main divisions between AI enthusiasts and many an argument is fought over which approach should prevail. Some people interested in AI believe that detailed understanding of human intelligence and behaviour is unnecessary because all we have to do is build the ideal learning machine, switch it on and let it learn! Others are of the opinion that this will take too long and anyway to build such a machine will require knowledge of how humans think. The argument is impossible to resolve and there is likely to be some truth in both points of view. Perhaps the more practical approach is to build and use anything that works, even if we don't know exactly how it works. After all, this is the approach inherent in the use of heuristics introduced in Chapters Two and Three.

Although programs and machines that learn are very much part of pattern recognition, learning is an interesting subject in its own right. First, it is worth looking at an example of the 'direct' recognition method and, then, look at the learning approach.

Recognising images

As already mentioned, pattern recognition started out from the desire to process visual patterns. To make significant headway in this sort of work, you need a television camera and an A-to-D convertor connected to a fairly fast computer. This tends to put pattern recognition out of the reach of most personal computer owners. However, if you are interested in pursuing the subject any further then it would be possible to build an image digitiser for around £500. Using a small array of light-sensitive diodes and a few lenses, it would be possible to construct a low-resolution visual input device for just tens of pounds. There are two types of visual image that you can try to recognise: two-tone (e.g. pure black and pure white) and 'full grey level' images, which are allowed the complete range of shades between these extremes. You can store a full grey level image using a two-dimensional array to store values that correspond to the brightness at each point. To recognise a pattern in a full grey level picture such as a photograph is much too complicated a problem from the hardware point of view, but we impose the restriction that the image to be analysed has only two tones, say black and white, then not only do the problems become easier to handle, we can do a certain amount of pattern recognition without any input device. The restriction to black and white images may seem like a major one but it is enough to deal with one of the most interesting and practically important pattern recognition problems: character recognition.

A black and white image can be input to a computer as an array of zeros and ones: a one representing black, say, and zero representing white. This is very much like the way computers such as the BBC Micro and the Spectrum specify their user-defined characters. Using this method it is possible to 'key in' black and white images as long as the number of black and white dots (usually called 'pixels' from 'picture elements') is kept small. For character recognition, this restriction is once again not too much of a problem as it is quite possible to represent a single character on an eight grid.

To summarise: visual images can be represented as a collection of values in a two-dimensional array, each value representing the brightness at a point in the image. For the sake of simplicity, it is useful to restrict consideration to images that have only two brightness values — black and white — these can be represented by a two-dimensional array holding only zeros and ones.

Recognising features

Consider the task of recognising a particular human face from a black and white photograph. If you were to reduce the photo to an array of numbers that was 'fine' enough to enable you still to recognise the face you would need an array of something like 1000 by 1000 or greater. This suggests that the recognition of a face or any other complex image depends on a judgement made on around one million or more brightness values. Processing this number of values obviously takes some time. Do humans really recognise faces etc in terms of the brightness values at a vast number of points? If you think about it for a while, you are likely to agree that faces are recognised in terms of 'features', e.g. type of hair, colour of eyes, shape of face etc. This is true of nearly all but the simplest recognition tasks. Complicated images are recognised in terms of the existence or the nature of a relatively small number of features.

This idea that recognition is based on 'features' is a very powerful one. In general, the problem of recognition can be broken down into two stages

```
          feature extraction     classification
image ─────────────────▶ features ─────────────▶ recognition
```

The first stage is feature extraction, e.g. working out the amount of hair a face has, then the second step is classifying the image on the basis of the features.

The only problem with this scheme is that, in general, the features that we use to recognise objects are unknown and at best they are only guessed at. How do we know that the shape of the face is a feature that we take into account when recognising a face? Perhaps it is the fact that we recognise the face that makes us see it as a different shape? Even though this problem exists, the idea of a feature is one of the most useful in pattern recognition and we shall return to it later.

Template matching

Rather than continue considering abstract ideas the time has come to think of practical things. Consider the problem of recognising the letters of the alphabet. A very simple scheme would be to set up a number of images corresponding to ideal examples of A to Z. Then when a new image was presented you could compare it to each of the 'prototypes' and classify it as the letter it was 'most like'. The only problems with this method are the setting up of the prototypes and deciding how to measure how alike two images are.

For the letters of the alphabet the problems of setting up prototypes is relatively easy. For example, we could define A as

```
00001000
00010100
00100010
00100010
00111110
00100010
00100010
00000000
```

and the other letters of the alphabet are equally straightforward. Measuring the similarity between images can be solved by using an idea from traditional statistics, the correlation coefficient. However, we can avoid any difficult mathematics by using a little common sense. If an image corresponds exactly with a prototype then it has ones in exactly the same places. We could measure the similarity between images by counting how many ones are in the same position in both images. There is another way to calculate the number of ones in the same position that at first sight seems a little 'round about' but makes a lot of sense later on. If you multiply the value at each pixel in the prototype by the value of the corresponding pixel in the prototype and add all the results up then this tells you how many ones are in the same place. In BASIC, assuming that the prototypes values are stored in the array M and the images in the array A, this is calculated by

```
R=0
FOR I=1 TO size of image
FOR J=1 TO size of image
R=R+M(I,J)*A(I,J)
NEXT I
NEXT J
```

This works because M(I,J)*A(I,J) is only if *both* pixels M(I,J) and A(I,J) are one. Adding the result of this multiplication for every pair of pixels gives a count of the number of places where the two images are both one.

This measure would be quite satisfactory except for one thing. It depends on the number of ones in the prototype. In fact, the maximum value it can reach is the number of ones in the prototype. Thus this measure of similarity takes into account not only how similar the two images are but how black and white they are overall. The solution to this problem is simple: take two more counts, one of the number of ones in the prototype and one of the number of ones in the image and use these to remove the dependence on the overall brightness. This is best done by using the following formula

$$\text{measure of similarity} = \frac{(\text{number of ones in the same place})^2}{(\text{number of ones in prototype})*(\text{number of ones in image})}$$

This formula may look a little complicated but, if you think about it a little, you should be able to understand what is going on. The most important thing to notice is that if the two images are the same then the measure of similarity given by this formula is equal to 1. Any disagreement between the two images reduces this value (For anyone interested in such things, this formula calculates the square of the correlation between the two images.)

This method of pattern recognition is usually called template matching. The prototypes are the templates and these are used to decide which class an image belongs to.

A letter recognition program

The following program is an example of template matching applied to character recognition. As it stands it can recognise the capital letter A from most others. If you want to, you could extend it to handle all the other letters of the alphabet.

```
10 DIM M(2,8,8)
20 DATA 00001000
30 DATA 00010100
40 DATA 00100010
50 DATA 00100010
60 DATA 00111110
70 DATA 00100010
80 DATA 00000000
500 DIM A(8,8)

1000 K=1
1010 GOSUB 2000
1020 GOSUB 3000
1030 GOSUB 4000
1040 K=1
1050 GOSUB 5000
1060 GOTO 1030

2000 FOR I=1 TO 8
2010 READ D
2020 FOR J=1 TO 8
2030 M(K,I,9-J)=D-INT(D/10)*10
2040 D=INT(D/10)
2050 NEXT J
2060 NEXT I
2070 RETURN

3000 PRINT "MASK ";K
3010 FOR I=1 TO 8
3020 FOR J=1 TO 8
3030 PRINT M(K,I,J);
3040 NEXT J
3050 PRINT
3060 NEXT I
3070 PRINT
3080 RETURN

4000 FOR I=1 TO 8
4010 PRINT "LINE ";I;
4020 INPUT LINE
4030 FOR J=1 TO 8
4040 A(I,9-J)=LINE-INT(LINE/10)*10
4050 LINE=INT(LINE/10)
4060 NEXT J
4070 NEXT I
4080 PRINT
4090 FOR I=1 TO 8
4100 FOR J=1 TO 8
4110 PRINT A(I,J);
4120 NEXT J
4130 NEXT I
4140 PRINT
4150 RETURN
```

Pattern recognition

```
5000 R=0
5010 C=0
5020 B=0
5030 FOR I=1 TO 8
5040 FOR J=1 TO 8
5050 R=R+M(K,I,J)*A(I,J)
5060 C=C+M(K,I,J)
5070 B=B+A(I,J)
5080 NEXT J
5090 NEXT I
5100 PRINT (R*R)/(C*B)
5110 RETURN
```

A three-dimensional array M is defined in line 10 and this is used to hold the templates. Although in this program only one template is stored [in M(1,I,J)] you could add others. The actual image that corresponds to the template for A is stored in the data statements 20–90. The array A is used to hold the test image. Subroutine 2000 reads the template definition into M. It should be easy to see how to change this to read in more than one template. Subroutine 3000 prints the pattern corresponding to any template according to the value of K, e.g. K=1 prints the first template. Subroutine 4000 accepts an image typed from the keyboard in the same eight by eight format that the template is in. The test image is also printed on the screen for the user to compare with the template. Finally subroutine 5000 computes the measure of similarity described in the last section.

Evaluating template matching

If you enter the 'perfect' letter A to the program you will see that the similarity reaches its maximum value 1. However, it is important to notice that 'perfect' simply means that the letter A is exactly the same as the template. If you look at Figure 6.1 you will see that the similarity of a letter B falls to 0.329 which probably means that it wouldn't be classified as a letter A! (i.e. it is almost certain to have a higher value when compared to the B template.) However, if you look at Figure 6.2 then you will see the result for a distorted A. The similarity at 0.62 is still higher than the result for the letter B it might not be enough to ensure that it is classified as an A.

Overall the template matching works surprisingly well for such a simple approach. However, the form that we are using does suffer from a major defect. Consider the output of the program to a

```
    00111110              00000000
    00100010              00000000
    00100010              00001000
    00111110              00011000
    00100010              00100010
    00100010              01000100
    00111110              01111110
    00000000              00100010

    result = 0.329        result = 0.6213

    Figure 6.1 Letter B   Figure 6.2 Distorted letter A
```

'perfect' letter A that is drawn 'hard' over to the left and at the bottom of the grid. It would have exactly the same shape as the letter A template but it wouldn't match perfectly because it would be in a slightly different place. Or for a more extreme example consider a letter A draw at an angle or even upside down; still the same shape but it would be considered a very poor match for the template!

Cross correlation

There are two possible solutions to the problem of the relative positions of the template and the image. Firstly, you could try to arrange for the input image to be in a fixed position and orientation. For example, you could arrange for all the input letters to be the right way up and in the middle of the array. This simple method doesn't work for very many problems because knowing which way up a letter is depends on knowing which letter it is and this of course is assuming the answer we are trying to reach!

A second and better solution is to work out the correlation between the image and a range of templates that represent the letter A at different orientations and positions and then take the maximum value as the measure of similarity. This seems quite reasonable from a common sense point of view in that if you want to know how similar an image is to a template then you should 'move it around' until it fits the image as well as it can. The series of values that you get for the correlation coefficent is technically known as the 'cross correlation' function but where this name comes from needn't worry us.

To summarise: the full template matching method is to calculate the correlation coefficient between the template and the image for every possible orientation and positional shift. The maximum value is then taken as the measure of how similar the two are and the image is classified as corresponding to the template that it is most like.

This method works very well with problems such as character recognition but in general it suffers from being too slow. After all, it takes a long time to work out the correlation between a pair of images for a wide range of orientations and positions. For character recognition the calculation can be speeded up quite a lot by assuming that all the characters are the right way up but even then the method is a little slow.

Features and grey levels

You may be wondering where all the discussion of features given earlier fits in to this simple template approach to pattern recognition? The answer is that each template corresponds to a feature! For example, the A template is used to measure a feature that might be called 'A-ness'. The higher the value of the similarity the more the image possesses A-ness! This description may seem a little odd in that we are trying to recognise the characters but suppose we were interested in recognising words that the letters made up. Any single word could be recognised by possessing a list of features each of which was a particular letter. In general, any pattern can be recognised by defining a number of templates corresponding to features that we are trying to detect. The final classification of the pattern would be made on the basis of which features were not present in the image.

Although you may think that this idea of template matching is limited by our earlier restriction to two-tone images, it is easily extended to include grey level images and even full colour images. All you have to do is carry out the same calculation that we did in the case of black and white images but allow them to take values other than zero and one. The resulting correlation coefficient still measures how similar the two images are and the final classification can still be made on the basis of which template the test image is closest to.

Features of recognition

The idea of a feature is so fundamental that it is difficult to imagine recognising patterns without a first stage of 'feature detection' or 'feature measurement'. The use of templates to recognise images is so straightforward and direct that it seems unnecessary to think of the results of matching a template to an image as measuring a feature of the image. This is even the case in the letter recognition problem because each of the templates represented one of the possible patterns, i.e. A to Z, in its entirety. The reason why recognition is so simple is that it is based on the presence or absence of a single feature. That is the letter A is recognised because it possesses more A-ness than B-ness, C-ness etc., (where A-ness is the degree to which it matches the A template and so on). In a more general problem, we would be faced with the difficulty of weighing up more than one feature. For example, when trying to recognise a London bus it is not enough to measure the feature 'colour' because this would lead us to confuse pillar boxes with buses! For a chance of correct classification we have at least to add to colour a measurement of height. However, you could still confuse a telephone kiosk with a bus!

The point is that most recognition problems involve weighing up the evidence of a number of features. So far, we have no way of approaching this more difficult problem.

Feature space

The key to understanding how we classify patterns when they possess more than one feature is contained in the expression 'weighing up the evidence'. This is in fact exactly what we, and computers' have to do! If you have made measurements on, say, two features of the pattern your problem is to reduce the two numbers to one single measurement indicating how like the ideal example of the pattern it is. Consider the problem a biologist faces when trying to identify which particular mammal a skull corresponds to. This is a real example because biologists often do want to identify what something has been eating from an examination of the skulls in its droppings. Two obvious features used in recognition are the length of the top of the skull and its maximum width. Roughly speaking, these two features represent the shape of the skull. If you wanted a finer distinction then you could always add more features but for simplicity we will stick at two. If you collect some measurements on two types of skull, otter and mink, say, then you will be faced with the problem of sorting out the meaning of columns of figures – never an easy task. The obvious thing to do is draw a plot of the measurements as shown in Figure 6.3. Each star on the graph indicates a pair of measurements on an otter and each circle indicates a pair of measurements made on a mink skull. If we are lucky then the two different types of animal will appear in 'clusters' on the diagram. In other words, there will be an area on the diagram where the otter skulls tend to fall and an area where the mink skulls tend to fall. You can see that this is the case in Figure 6.3. If this grouping doesn't occur, there is nothing that can be done about it; it merely indicates that the features that we are measuring do not contain enough information to distinguish the two types of objects. However, if the two groups are well separated we could use this fact to classify any new object. By making measurements of the two features, a new object can be added to the diagram. If we don't know which of the two groups it

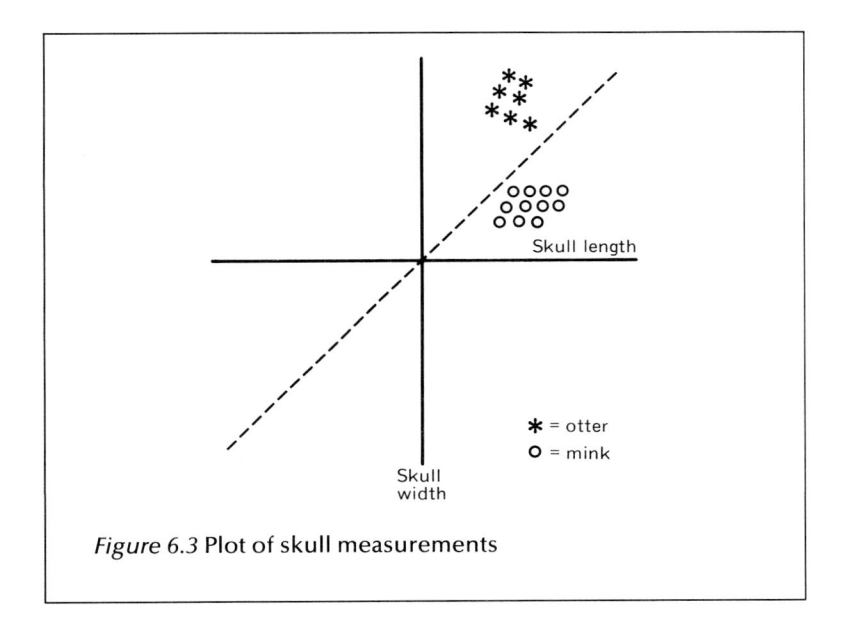

Figure 6.3 Plot of skull measurements

belongs to it seems reasonable to suppose that it is an example of whichever group it is closest to on the diagram. This is indeed a very sensible idea and results in a good rate of correct recognition but it can hardly be called an easy method to apply.

If we are lucky enough to find two features that separate the two groups sufficiently to draw a line between them then we could use an alternative method of deciding which group a new object is an example of. We could simply suppose that the new object was an example of the group that was on the same side of the line.

All that we have to do to turn this into a workable method is to translate it into mathematics. If we denote the two feature measurements by X1 and X2, then the side of the line that the point falls is given by the sign of W1*X1 + W2*X2. The point falls on one side of the line if this quantity is positive and on the other side if it is negative. You may be wondering what W1 and W2 are? The answer is the values of W1 and W2 define the position and orientation of the line. As we vary the values of W1 and W2 the line moves around the diagram. Obviously to make use of the above equation to classify a new object we must first find the values of W1 and W2 that correspond to the line that best divides the two groups. This may seem a little complicated but if we suppose that the line that best separates the two groups corresponds to values of W1=2 and W2=−2 then a measurement of X1=3 and X2=2 would give W1*X1+W2*X2 a positive value (of 2). This would mean that the object that gives rise to the measurements X1 and X2 would be classified as an example of the group on the positive side of the line.

To recapitulate:

(1) If you plot a diagram of some examples of measurements of objects from two groups you might find that the measurements cluster in such a way that the groups can be separated by drawing a line between them.
(2) The line that best separates the groups can be expressed mathematically in such a way that it corresponds to particular values of two constants W1 and W2.
(3) New objects can be classified or recognised by working out W1*X1+W2*X2 which indicates whether the point falls on the 'positive' or 'negative' side of the line.

The one big question left unanswered is *how* do you find the line that best separates the groups. There are methods that can determine the best line in one (rather complicated) calculation but these methods are more part of statistical theory rather than AI and pattern recognition. The method that we are interested in leads us to a possible general approach to learning to recognise.

Finding a line by learning

For a moment, let us suppose that we have measurements on examples from two groups. If we give some arbitrary values to W1 and W2, we could work out W1*X1+W2*X2 for each object in the set of examples. If we also make the arbitrary decision that group 1 is on the positive side of the line and group 2 is on the negative side, we can compare the predictions of our arbitrary dividing line with

Pattern recognition

the groups that each object actually comes from. The results that we get are unlikely to be very good. After all assigning arbitrary values to W1 and W2 corresponds to just drawing any old line across the diagram! However, by using the results of how well or how badly the objects are classified we can try to adjust the values of W1 and W2 to improve the result (see Figure 6.4). This is what learning is all about! Let's look at this idea in more detail.

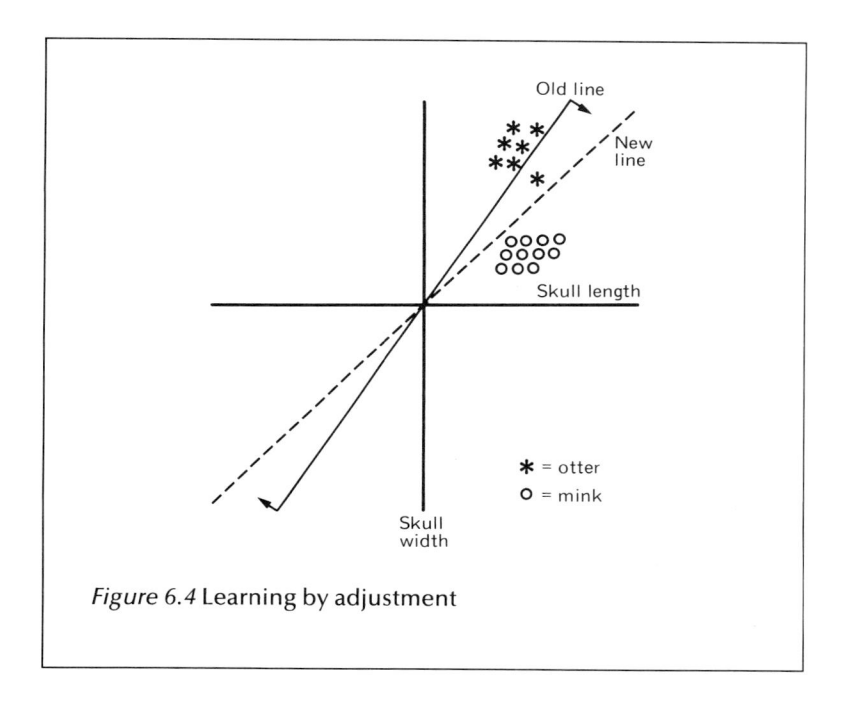

Figure 6.4 Learning by adjustment

If we work out W1*X1+W2*X2 for a particular object and find that it is classified correctly then the values that W1 and W2 currently have are OK for this object. If, however, it is classified into the wrong group then some adjustment of the values of W1 and W2 would be a good idea. There are many ways of adjusting W1 and W2 but all of them involve moving the line that W1 and W2 correspond to so that the misclassified point is closer to the correct side of the line. The simplest rule is to move the line a fixed amount in the direction that places the misclassified object closer to its correct side. Mathematically, this correction is worked out in the following way:

(1) If the object is really in group 1 (the positive group) then

W1(new)=W1 + a*X1
W2(new)=W2 + a*X2

and if the object is really in group 2 (the negative group) then

W1(new)=W1 − a*X1
W2(new)=W2 − a*X2

where 'a' is a constant that controls the rate at which the objects are 'learned'.

(2) If the adjustment is carried out for each of the objects that we have then, hopefully, if we repeat the whole process once more the classification performance will have improved. If we keep on repeating the process eventually we will reach a point where no improvement is possible: we have learned to recognise the set of objects. If a new object arrives and we do not know which group it belongs to the final values of W1 and W2 can be used to attempt a classification.

The process described above, although fairly simple, has all the elements of learning. The initial set of objects with known identity are used as a 'training set'. The classifier, or recogniser, given by W1*X2 + W2*X2 is 'taught' to recognise each of the known objects by attempting a classification and then being corrected. Once the training set is learned, the recogniser can be put to good use classifying unknown objects. This sort of learning is often called 'supervised learning' because of the need for a 'teacher' to adjust the values of W1 and W2 during training. Unsupervised learning, i.e. dispensing with the teacher, is possible and will be described later.

All of the ideas described so far can be extended to the case where more than two features are measured. For example, in the case of three features the classification is given by

W1*X1 + W2*X2 + W3*X3

In general N features will need N values of W. Another way of thinking about the W values and the way they are used is as 'weighting' factors. The size and sign of each W governs how much importance is given to each feature in recognising an object.

You may also be wondering what happens if there are more than two groups of objects to be recognised. The answer is that they are taken two at a time!

The Perceptron

The description of learning given above is based upon the idea that features are measured and then a recogniser is trained. If you have

Pattern recognition

chosen the features well then everything will work as described. But how do you choose the features? What happens if you don't choose good features? Questions such as these are very difficult to answer in general. It does seem to be avoiding the real issue to use a human to pick the features that a recogniser uses! There is a way of allowing a program or a machine to pick its own features but before examining this idea we must extend the definition of 'feature'. So far 'feature' has been taken to mean a measurement that 'makes sense' to a human. Why should features that are used to recognise patterns make sense to a human? Perhaps all the features that we claim to use are just rationalisations covering up what we really use! Certainly deep down inside our brains there are more primitive features that are used to recognise things that do not really correspond to things that we can put a name to. This more general idea of a feature might be easier to understand after the description of a machine (or a program) that constructs its own features: the Perceptron.

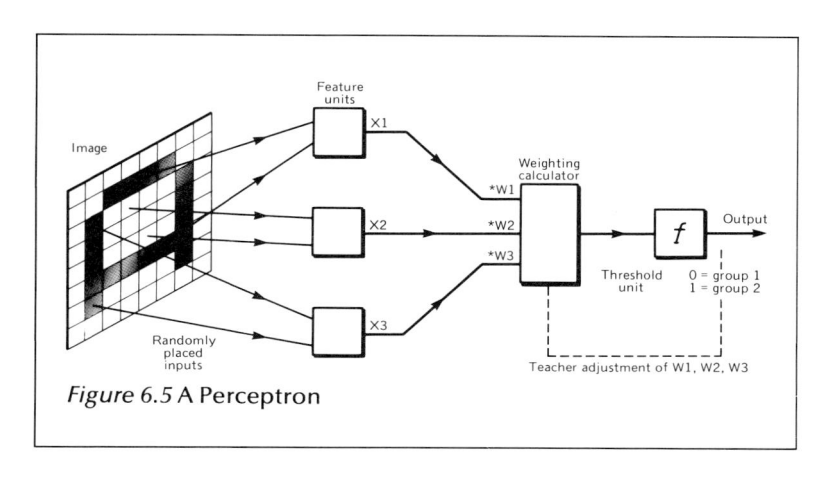

Figure 6.5 A Perceptron

The Perceptron is a learning recogniser that works in a very similar way to the supervised learning program described earlier. The output from a number of feature measuring devices is fed into a unit that calculates the equivalent of W1*X1+W2*X2 etc. The output from this unit is then fed to a threshold unit which in effect makes the decision about which group the pattern belongs to. All this can be seen in Figure 6.5. What is different about the Perceptron is the way that the features are selected and measured. If you look at Figure 6.5, you will see that each of the feature measuring devices takes the form of a number of connections that measure the brightness at points on the image. These measurements are processed to yield a single 0 or 1 result by adding them together and once again using a threshold unit. The effect is that the output of the threshold unit is 1 if a particular pattern is present at each of the connection points and 0 otherwise. The actual locations of the connections are arbitrary. In fact, it is an advantage if they are randomly assigned over the entire pattern. A Perceptron would have to be trained by exposing it to a training set before it would be of any use. As the training progresses, some of the outputs from the feature units will be ignored by virtue of their W values being set to zero or very near zero. The useful features will be those with W values other than zero. As you might imagine because the features are random *most* of them are not useful! To overcome this problem, a real Perceptron has to have a very large number (200 plus) of feature units to increase the chances of finding a few good features! This may sound crude but is probably very close to the way that the human brain learns. After all, there are enough neurons to waste a few!

The Perceptron is a useful example of a learning machine. It has received a great deal of criticism in academic circles but it is still a good way of doing things. Perceptron-like programs and hardware are used in some commercial pattern recognition machines. They are the main component in speech recognisers where the input pattern consists of the amount of power in a number of frequency bands. This accounts for the fact that speech recognition add-ons have to be taught the words that they are to recognise.

There is one point left to discuss. The learning methods that we have considered are supervised methods that demand a teacher who knows all the right answers during the training phase. This corresponds to some human learning situations but certainly not all. Somehow we sometimes manage to learn without a teacher. A little thought quickly shows that this is not magic. A human is different from the simple machines that we have been discussing in that a human *acts* on the results of his recognition. By observing the further results of the actions it is normally possible to decide if the recognition was correct or not and so adjust the recognition method. For example, if you think you recognise a London bus and jump aboard what turns out to be a stationary pillar box (!!!) you will presumably add size as well as colour to your list of bus recognition features. Until AI machines become a little more adventurous, learning machines will need teachers to evaluate their decisions.

If you think that the Preceptron is a very limited form of recogniser then I would tend to agree with you. It is difficult to imagine a single Perceptron capable of recognising a particular human face, but then why restrict ourselves to a single Perceptron? A really sophisticated recognition machine would use many 'banks' of Perceptrons. Each bank would feed its outputs to the next bank as detected features. As the amount of processing increased, the features that one bank fed to another would become increasingly complicated and more like the sort of features that humans give names to. For example, the first bank may detect lines in an image, the second bank angles and connected lines, a much later bank would detect squares and other shapes and so on. But all this is well beyond the range of the microcomputer!

Uses of pattern recognition

Sometimes the recognition of patterns is an end in its own right. For example, letter recognition is a useful and important pattern recognition problem because, if you can recognise letters, you can dispense with all of the work involved in transferring existing printed text to computers. In the same way, speech recognition is a useful facility even if it isn't used in conjunction with any other intelligent software. These and other important recognition problems have tended to emphasise pattern recognition as a subject in its own right with few connections with the rest of AI. However it seems reasonable to suppose that this will change as acceptable solutions are found to the simpler pattern recognition problems. The subjects of artificial vision and hearing are clearly important for a complete and satisfying solution to the more general AI problem and the emphasis is bound to shift to the interaction between AI and pattern recognition. There is another side to pattern recognition that is less obvious but equally important to AI. For example, one of the problems in implementing rule-based knowledge systems is recognising the 'condition' that is part of the IF...THEN rule. In the examples given in Chapter Four the 'condition' was easy to detect or recognise but, as programs that reason move into more complicated areas, pattern recognition methods are going to become increasingly important in this process. AI programs of the future are going to have to include a stage of pattern recognition to provide the data that they work with.

7

Language

If you think about it for a moment, it should be obvious that computers actually spend more time processing text – the written word – than they do crunching numbers. The interesting thing is that this processing of text for the most part only takes the form of moving characters from one place to another. In other words, nearly all close encounters between computers and languages are very little more than storage and retrieval. The ultimate goal is, of course, to improve this state of affairs to the point where computers show a degree of understanding of everyday human language. The first computers that manage this will be large and will be found mainly in research centres. However, when the future equivalent of today's micros possess this ability the world of computing will be *very* different.

Looking into the future is fun and can even be useful in that it can help prepare the way for new uses of computers. However, there is a great deal more that can be done with text as language using fairly straightforward methods that are available on even the smallest micro. To a certain extent, what is actually done with computers is a matter of what is necessary. Text processors are a very obvious and lucrative use of computers but it took a surprisingly long time before anyone thought of writing spelling or grammar correction programs. There seems to be a barrier that faces programmers whenever they think in terms of language processing. Handling language is difficult if your goal is complete understanding but there are many easier useful goals on the way. Language can appear to be very technical with the old school subject of grammar rearing its frightening head. However, apart from a certain amount of new jargon there is nothing to be frightened of!

Syntax and semantics

There are two components to language, the way it is written − its syntax − and the meaning it contains − its semantics. Of these two components, syntax is the easier to deal with but also the less interesting. However, understanding syntax is necessary before you can understand the meaning of language. Also, for many practical purposes, understanding syntax is enough to extract the approximate meaning.

The subject of syntax is by no means new. It has been studied for years under the name of grammar at levels ranging from school English lessons to pure research. The first myth that it is important to dispel is that there is an exact or rigorous set of rules that form the Grammar of the English language. There is nothing so straightforward ! English, along with most other languages, is sufficiently subtle to make any simple set of rules insufficient to describe all the ways there are of saying things. Another important idea is that not everything that obeys even the simplest rules of grammar makes sense. For example,

> The dream sleeps furiously

is a correctly formed English sentence. It has a noun, a verb and even an adverb but it makes little sense. 'Dream' is a noun but it is not something that can 'sleep'. 'Sleep' is a verb but 'furiously' is not an adverb that can sensibly be applied to it. In short, a correct sentence but nonsense! This should illustrate that syntax and semantics are separate components of language.

Describing syntax

Before it is possible to analyse a particular sentence it is necessary to find a way of describing the ways that words can be put together. For example,

> mat the on sat cat

can be recognised as a mangled version of a familiar English sentence but it is obvious that it is not English. What rules this sentence out is actually something simpler than it not making sense. It is that it breaks some simple rules about the order in which words can be put together in a sentence. The important observation here is that, although there can be syntax without semantics, there can be no semantics without syntax.

Although it is difficult to find a complete set of rules that describe the English language it is possible to make a start on the problem.

For example, a typical sentence has the form

> noun phrase verb phrase

In other words, most English sentences are about something – the subject of the noun phrase – doing something, the action in the verb phrase. In the sentence

> He jumped

'He' is the noun phrase and 'jumped' is the verb phrase. Things can be more complicated than this, however, because noun and verb phrases can be more than one word long. What we need is to produce some rules to govern the way that such phrases can be produced. If a sentence is then made up by joining two correct phrases together in the right order, it is also correct. For example, a noun phrase can be constructed as follows:

> Article adjectives noun

where article is one of a fairly short list of words like 'a', 'the' or 'some', and an adjective describes the noun it is associated with. Using this we can now extend the example sentence to

> The big man jumped

One way of 'seeing' the structure of a sentence and the rules that it follows is to use our old friend the tree diagram again.

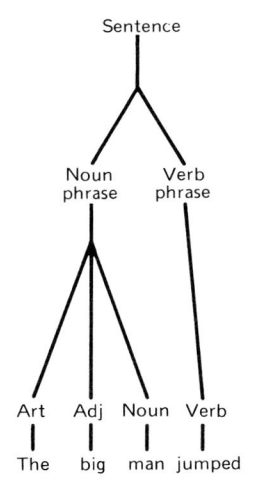

```
                    Sentence
                   /        \
              Noun           Verb
              phrase         phrase
             /  |  \           |
           Art Adj Noun       Verb
            |   |   |          |
           The big man       jumped
```

Using this diagram you can see how this simple sentence is built up. Notice that it is only at the very bottom level of the tree that actual words appear. At all the other levels, the labels that appear are descriptions of a part of speech.

Parsing

Understanding the syntax of a sentence can be thought of as trying to find the syntax tree that describes it. This is known as 'parsing' the sentence and is a prerequisite to understanding the sentence. In general, parsing an English sentence is very difficult and can only be accomplished by a step-by-step testing of possibilities. This is much too large a task for a micro running BASIC. One approach to parsing is to start at the top of the syntax tree and try to match the different parts of speech against the sentence; this is known as 'top-down parsing'. As you might imagine, the opposite approach, starting at the bottom and working up, is known as 'bottom-up' parsing. The reason why parsing is difficult is that there are so many possibilities to try out. Even fitting the bottom level of the tree is a large task. For example, you need a list of all the nouns and verbs that the program is likely to meet, let alone all the adjectives and adverbs.

On a more positive note, it is worth mentioning that computer languages are much simpler and many compilers begin the problem of translating high level language to machine code by parsing each statement of the program.

Generating language

The importance of syntax trees for the small computer is more to do with generating correct sentences. Syntax trees are ideal from the point of view of making the syntax of a sentence clear to a human but computers do not find diagrams quite so helpful! To overcome the difficulty a non-graphical way of representing the rule of syntax has to be found. The most commonly used solution is based on the idea of a 'production rule'. So far we have the following rules for a simple sentence:

S→Noun phrase Verb phrase
Noun phrase→article adjective noun
Verb phrase→verb

where the '→' can be read as 'is a'. These rules are called production rules because they show how one element of syntax can be 'produced' from another.

There are a number of problems with this notation. The first is that it is difficult to distinguish between things that are further defined later on and things that are replaced by actual words. For example, Noun Phrase has a further definition to come but noun or verb are final and have to be replaced by representative words from each class. To make this difference clear angle brackets <> can be used to indicate an item that has a further definition. A second problem is that a part of speech such as a noun phrase may have a number of alternative definitions. This problem can be solved by using a vertical bar | to mean 'choose one of'. For example,

    <noun phrase>→ pronoun|article adjective noun

which means that a <noun phrase> can be either a pronoun such as 'he' or 'she' etc or as described in the earlier examples. A better illustration is provided by a fuller definition of <verb phrase>

    <verb phrase>→verb adverb|null <PP>

This means that a <verb phrase> is a verb such as 'jump' etc and either an adverb or 'null'. Using 'null' is just a way of saying that you can either have an adverb following the verb or not! The interesting extra element is <PP> standing for 'prepositional phrase'. The definition of <PP> is

    <PP>→preposition <noun phrase> <PP>|null

The first part of the definition is straightforward in that a preposition is something like 'on', 'under', 'to' etc but the rest of the definition is interesting. The occurrence of <noun phrase> in the definition is surprising enough but <PP> occurring in its own definition...! The secret of understanding this seeming contradiction is the '|null' part. All this sort of definition means is that you can have as many <PP>s in a sentence as you like. It means that if you want to follow a 'preposition <noun phrase>' by another then you can do so or you can select the 'null' and so finish the <PP>. As an example of this more elaborate sort of <verb phrase>, consider the correct version of the mangled sentence quoted earlier.

    Tha cat sat on the mat

In this case the <verb phrase> is 'sat on the mat'. The verb is 'sat' the <PP> is 'on the mat'. This splits down into the preposition 'on' and the <noun phrase> 'the mat'. The resulting syntax tree can be seen in Figure 7.1.

Using this set of definitions it is possible to write a program that can generate fairly convincing English text. The algorithm of the program is closely related to the syntax definitions. In fact, it is so closely related that it is quite possible to write a program that will read in a list of syntax definitions and generate meaningful sentences that are correct according to the rules of the syntax. However, this is a slightly more ambitious program than the one considered below.

The basic principle that lies behind the sentence-generating program is that the sentence is built up from left to right and there is

Language

Figure 7.1 Syntax tree for 'The cat sat on the mat'

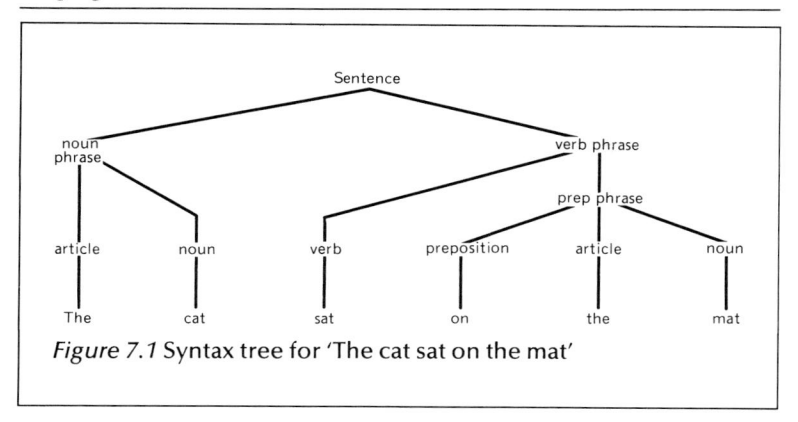

a subroutine corresponding to every item enclosed in angle brackets. Each subroutine either calls another subroutine, supplies a word of the correct type or does nothing, which is the programs equivalent of a null.

The computer chat program

A small program that uses the syntax rules given above is presented here. The syntax rules themselves are collected together in Table 7.1.

TABLE 7.1.

<SENTENCE> → <NOUN PHRASE> <VERB PHRASE>

<NOUN PHRASE> → ARTICLE PHRASE

<VERB PHRASE> → VERB ADVERB | <PP> | NULL

<PP> → PREPOSITION <NOUN PHRASE>

You may find it surprising that the program is so short. The main reason for this is its small vocabulary, only 19 words! Even so it is quite fun to read what it has to say. Two examples of its output are

   The tiny bug runs to the big computer

and

   A tiny computer prints quickly under a big computer

neither of which is very deep, although they both have a certain naive charm.

```
10 GOSUB 1000
20 GOSUB 2000
30 GOSUB 3000
40 PRINT S$
50 STOP

1000 ART=2
1010 DIM A$(ART)
1020 A$(1)="A"
1030 A$(2)="THE"

1100 NOUN=4
1110 DIM N$(NOUN)
1120 N$(1)="COMPUTER"
1130 N$(2)="PRINTER"
1140 N$(3)="PROGRAM"
1150 N$(4)="BUG"

1200 ADJ=3
1210 DIM D$(ADJ)
1220 D$(1)="BIG"
1230 D$(2)="POOR"
1240 D$(3)="TINY"

1300 VERB=4
1310 DIM V$(VERB)
1320 V$(1)="WRITES"
1330 V$(2)="RUNS"
1340 V$(3)="DEBUGS"
1350 V$(4)="PRINTS"

1400 ADVERB=3
1410 DIM B$(ADVERB)
1420 B$(1)="SLOWLY"
1430 B$(2)="FAST"
1440 B$(3)="QUICKLY"

1500 PREP=3
1510 DIM P$(PREP)
1520 P$(1)="ON"
1530 P$(2)="TO"
1540 P$(3)="UNDER"

1600 S$=""
1610 RETURN

2000 REM NOUN PHRASE
2010 REM ARTICLE
2020 S$=S$+" "+A$(INT(RND(0)*ART)+1)
2030 REM ADJECTIVE/NULL
2040 IF RND(0)>.5 THEN S$=S$+" "+
     D$(INT(RND(0)*ADJ)+1)
2050 REM NOUN
2060 S$=S$+" "+N$(INT(RND(0)*NOUN)+1)
2070 RETURN
```

```
3000 REM VERB PHRASE
3010 REM VERB
3020 S$=S$+" "+V$(INT(RND(0)*VERB)+1)
3030 REM ADVERB/NULL
3040 IF RND(0)>.5 THEN S$=S$+" "+
     B$(INT(RND(0)*ADVERB)+1)
3050 GOSUB 4000
3060 RETURN

4000 REM PROPOSITIONAL PHRASE
4010 REM OR NULL
4020 IF RND(0)>.5 THEN RETURN
4030 REM PROPOSITION
4040 S$=S$+" "+P$(INT(RND(0)*PREP)+1)
4050 REM NOUN PHRASE
4060 GOSUB 2000
4070 RETURN
```

Subroutine 1000 sets up the word lists. There is an array for every type of word used in a sentence. It is easy to add further words to extend the vocabulary of the program but take care that the words go into the correct list! Subroutine 2000 constructs a noun phrase by extracting a word at random from the article list, selecting optionally from the adjective list and then selecting from the noun list. Subroutine 3000 works in roughly the same way except that it calls subroutine 4000 to supply a prepositional phrase. If a prepositional phrase is required then subroutine 2000 is called again to provide another noun phrase. This re-use of subroutine 2000 shows the power of the overall method of writing subroutines to generate each part of speech. Subroutine 2000 generates a <noun phrase> whether it is needed either directly or as part of a phrase being generated by another subroutine.

As with all the examples in this book, this program has been written in Microsoft BASIC, which should make it easy to convert to other BASICs. Although good fun, it is far from a final version and is really only a starting point for your experiments with generating readable text. Try to extend the vocabulary and the syntax rules so that the sentences produced make better sense. As an exercise you could try to improve the program to the point where you could fool someone into thinking that a human had written the output! A more useful idea is to try to produce a program that would generate short poems or something similar.

Syntax and meaning

Syntax is about the way that words can be put together to form correct English. Semantics is about the meaning contained within the correct English. Although language can be generated using production rules, there is no suggestion that there is any meaning contained in the words thus produced. When the 'Computer Chat' program prints a sentence on the screen, it is obvious that this is no attempt at communication by your computer. For example, the Computer Chat program can easily produce a sentence like

   The program runs slowly

When this appears on your computer's screen it does not mean that your computer doesn't think much of your program − or does it?

Innocent meaning

If you take the time and trouble to increase the vocabulary and the syntax rules used by the Computer Chat program you can make it produce a wide range of natural-sounding language. If you then sit a complete innocent down in front of a running Computer Chat program, their reaction will depend on what they have been told about computers in the past. However, you are very likely to come across a number of people who begin to read the output of Computer Chat as if it contained meaning and, in no time at all, the computer running the program begins to take on the personality of a rather confused and slightly demented human trapped inside a box with a lot of electronics!

   The point is that, to anyone who understands the method that Computer Chat uses to produce language, the sentences obviously lack any meaning but humans are very good at reading meaning into things even when there is none. The result of this tendency to find meaning is that it is very easy to fool an naive user into believing that computers are more capable than they truly are. It's a good job that AI experts are in general an honest bunch because it would be relatively easy for them to fool people (including other AI experts) that they had achieved more than they really had!

   It is obvious that we need to look a little more carefully at what makes language meaningful but first it is worth taking another look at methods for generating correct language.

Approximations to language

For the time being, let's forget that we know anything about syntax and try to find other ways of generating language. You could begin by writing a BASIC program that produced the letters of the

Language

alphabet completely at random. If you looked at the output of such a program you might spot the occasional word but mostly you would find nonsense. To improve the number of correct words found the most obvious thing to do is to alter the frequency that each letter is used. For example, there is little point in generating as many letter Zs as letter As since there is not very much use of the letter 'Z' in normal English. The best thing to do is to adjust the frequency that each letter is used until it is the same as the frequency that each letter occurs in normal English. To improve the performance further it is also necessary to ensure that pairs of letters occur with the same frequency that they do in normal English. After pairs of letters come triplets of letters, quadruplets etc. Each time you control the frequency of a larger group of letters the generated language becomes closer to correct English.

The importance of this idea is that you can clearly see that it is possible to produce better and better approximations to language without knowing anything about its syntax or semantics. All you have to do is collect a lot of examples and count the frequencies of occurrence of groups of letters – a job that can be made a lot easier by using a computer! What then is the purpose of studying syntax if a simple random scheme can also produce correct language?

Meaning from syntax

The value of knowing about syntax comes not from the ability to produce correct language but from the way that it provides a 'guide' to the meaning of a sentence. If you have a sentence and can identify its syntax then you have a 'map' which you can use to investigate its meaning. If a sentence is of the form 'NOUN PHRASE' 'VERB PHRASE' then you know that it's telling you what the object in 'NOUN PHRASE' is doing, i.e. the action in 'VERB PHRASE'. By knowing what type of sentence you are dealing with you can select the appropriate 'next action' However, as explained earlier, the task of discovering the syntax, or parsing, a sentence is too demanding for BASIC.

There is an even more serious defect with this proposed scheme. Apart from a very small part of English, there is no exact grammar or syntax of the form that we have been discussing. There are many extensions to the simple syntax trees that we have been looking at but so far the complexity of human language is still more than we can describe.

Practical understanding

If this last paragraph has depressed you then take heart because with a little courage and a lot of effort it is possible to write programs that have a limited amount of understanding and also respond appropriately. The key is not to aim too high and always to remember that there must be a human somewhere in the system willing to help a feeble and sometimes misunderstanding computer.

This is too ambitious a project for an example program and, as already mentioned, BASIC isn't really suitable for such a task. However, with the knowledge that you already have you should be able to understand how such a limited program could be written. For example, suppose you wanted to write a program that supplied the time and some route information for a number of bus services. For the 'human interface' part of the program you could use the traditional approach of supplying a 'menu' of options and then asking questions such as 'which bus number ?' and 'what is your destination code ?'. This is an easy approach because it avoids handling words in the responses supplied by the user but it strengthens the belief of 'the man in the street' that computers can only handle numbers! A slightly more ambitious approach would be to allow the user to 'converse' with the program using a restricted but natural sort of English. The way that this would be achieved is to think of the possible range of sentences that a user might type at the terminal and construct a small set of syntax rules that will generate them. A common question would be

What time is the next bus

This could be described by the syntax

<Query> is the <bus description>

The item <Query> might be expanded to include things like 'when' or even 'where'. The <bus description> could be further defined to include different ways of specifying which bus was being asked about. By matching what the user types in to a list of possible syntax diagrams, the program can determine what response to give. That is, if a sentence typed in by the user matches the syntax given above the program should give the time of the bus specified. This scheme is not too difficult but it does need a medium sized computer and a reasonable amount of memory to handle the vocabulary. (This approach to understanding is known as 'pragmatic syntax').

Good will and understanding: Eliza

To round off this introduction to computers and language it is worth looking at a program that achieved a certain amount of notoriety, Eliza. Not too long ago during the early experiments with language and AI, a program was written that could carry on reasonably good conversations with human beings on a variety of topics. The program was called Eliza after the famous character in Shaw's play 'Pygmalion'. The way it worked was fairly simple. It detected the presence of certain 'keywords' and by changing the tense and extracting clauses from the user's input it was able to 'turn' sentences round and 'fire' them back at the user. The most successful version of this program would talk about any personal problems that you might have (or pretend to have) and was therefore called 'Eliza Doctor'. Although the program was very simple it had a large vocabulary and this combined with the way that humans 'read meaning' into things made it very convincing. It was so convincing that 'real' patients and 'real' doctors started using it. Indeed it was so good that some patients preferred it to a human doctor!! The program's creator and many other AI experts were very worried by how easy it was to make a large number of ordinary and well-educated people have long and intimate conversations with a completely unintelligent program!

The principles that Eliza uses are very easy to describe. Firstly it scans any input for certain 'keywords'. On detecting one of these keywords its action is always the same. It either prints a standard message or it uses part of the input to construct a message. For example, if you were to type

> I hate icecream

it would detect the keyword 'hate' and would respond with

> It is not good to hate.

Notice that it will produce this response irrespective of the rest of the sentence. If this is all the Eliza did it would be very easy to spot that it was a program by the limited range of responses it produced. However, to introduce some variety into its responses it can make use of the input sentence. Any sentence that the user types in is scanned for the occurrence of certain words or phrases such as 'my' or 'you are'. If any of these are found then they are changed into the appropriate 'opposite' e.g. 'my' is changed to 'your' and 'you are' is changed to 'I am'. The purpose of this simple change is that input sentences can then be printed back at the user as if they are originated by the program. For example, if you type in

> You are an idiot

This is changed to

> I am an idiot

which the program can simply print back at the user with perhaps the addition of a few exclamation or question marks.

These two techniques — keyword response and tense changing — added to a few other specialised tricks can produce a program that will carry on a reasonable conversation with you. BASIC Eliza programs are available which are only a few pages long — another testament to how willing we are to lend computers our intelligence. The moral of the story is everything that talks to you isn't necessarily understanding you...!!!

More language in programs

Language is a different area but with a little more willingness and a certain amount of trial and error quite a lot more can be done than you find in today's crop of applications programs. Take a second look at any medium-sized programs that you are responsible for and try to see the opportunities for language input and output within them and then try to implement your ideas. You will find the necessary string handling tedious and the program will grow in size but you will be surprised at just how far you can get with pragmatic grammar and Eliza-like techniques. If after implementing your design you then test it by allowing other people to use it you are bound to find ways in which your pragmatic syntax fails. By taking notice of these failures it should be easy to change your program to cope with them. By repeated testing and improvement, you should be able to produce a program that understands a restricted but adequate subset of English without having to solve the entire AI natural language problem!

8

Approaching intelligence

One of the fascinating things about AI is the way that the same method, or program, can be described, or thought of, in more than one way. This fascination can be something of a problem in that it is often difficult to work out what is really new! You can look at a program that solves some problem and not realise that it is far from new simply because it is explained in terms that are unfamiliar. Perhaps the single most important theme of this book has been that there is nothing very different about intelligent programs and that they can be understood without any difficult theory. However, to a certain extent this practical approach misses some of the central philisophical issues of AI. For while it is clear that computers can mimic some of the aspects of intelligent behaviour the answer to questions like 'can a computer be intelligent?' or 'can a computer become aware or have a personality?' are entirely open!

In this last chapter, the discussion is widened to include not just the practical aspects of current AI but some of the more philosophical points. You may feel that the last chapter is a little late to be considering the question of whether or not AI can ever achieve its long-term goal but its not until you have experienced some of the methods that current AI uses, and understood how simple they really are, can you appreciate just how far away the ultimate goal really is! However, before examining these wider questions, it is worth examining some of the alternative and auxiliary approaches to the study of intelligence.

The biological approach

The earlier chapters of this book have tended to view the AI problem as a branch of engineering. It is not at all obvious that this approach is the best one because the only good examples of working intelligent systems that we have are biological in nature. There is another approach to AI that is more closely connected to biology. The only trouble is that this approach has never really been gathered together under the heading of a single discipline. Some of the work in this area concentrates on studying the way that the human, and other animal, brain works and is generally included under neurophysiology, if it involves examining the physical structures of the brain, and psychology otherwise.

Much of what these two subjects have to say is relevant to AI and can provide a great deal of background material but it is very rarely of direct use. The difficulty is that neurophysiology provides information that, at the moment at least, explains in great detail how small collections of neurons work. If you try an use these explanations as a way of implementing AI systems it nearly always proves that there is a simpler way of obtaining the same result. For example, from neurophysiology, we know that there are groups of neurons in the visual centres of the cat's brain that detect small line segments. The way that this is achieved is interesting but we can construct line detectors that are just as efficient without using artificial neurons. In other words, neurophysiology tells us how simple things are achieved using a completely different technology! In the same way, psychology tells us things that are far too general about the way that animals and humans behave. It is rare for psychology to describe *how* something works in enough detail for it to be useful in AI.

It is important to realise that just because neurophysiology and psychology have as yet failed to come up with anything that can be used in AI programs, there is no reason to think that they never will! It is essential to study and learn from the biological implementations of intelligence all around us.

Cybernetic systems

Cybernetics is a discipline that tries to study biological systems from the point of view of engineering. The overall cybernetic approach is difficult to define but its practitioners tend to adopt the attitude that there is really no difference between machines that are implemented in the 'soft' technology of cells etc and the 'hard' technology of silicon, the main thing is that they are all machines. This idea is really nothing more than a philosophical point but it tends to concentrate attention on the principles involved rather than the details of how they are implemented. Cybernetics started off by examining the mechanisms that control the simpler aspects of living systems. For example, somehow your body manages to maintain a fairly steady temperature even if the external temperature is fluctuating. This is clearly not intelligent behaviour but at the time when cybernetics was just beginning the principles behind such regulation were very poorly understood. Today the fundamental principle of self-regulation – feedback – is well known, and indeed important, in many branches of engineering. Feedback is a foundation without which the more interesting and sophisticated forms of intelligent behaviour would not exist. For example, if you try to pick something up off a table the muscles in your arm are controlled by nerve impulses from your brain. The simplest strategy is in some way to 'measure' where the object is, work out what impulses to send to the arm, send them and then wait until the arm reaches its destination. This is indeed the strategy used by many mechanical robots and its deficiency becomes obvious if the object on the table is moved while the arm is in motion! To try and pick up an object that might move, you have to keep measuring its position and comparing it with the current position of the arm. What happens when you pick up an object is that the difference between your hand and the object is used by the brain to work out how to move your arm so as to reduce the difference. Of course the move is complete only when the difference is reduced to zero and this takes care of any movement that the object might make. The basic mechanism involved in picking up an object can be found as part of many other functions of a living system. This is 'feedback control', the essence of which is the way that the system measures a difference, or error quantity, and then tries to reduce it.

Although feedback is a simple idea it can become very involved in practice. Now much of cybernetics is involved in studying the wider implications of feedback and other aspects of self-regulating systems. For example, what characterises a system that can organise itself, repair itself or reproduce? The question of whether the success of feedback control as an explanation of self-regulation can be extended or replaced by a new theory is something that only time will tell.

In the early days of AI there was much more emphasis on hardware. It was supposed that intelligence would need new types of machine. Today it is widely recognised that new machines are only needed to make programs run faster. So far there has been no great machine creation that has added anything new. The rule seems to be that if it can be done, it can be implemented in either software or hardware and hardware is more expensive but more efficient. However, this said it is important to realise that by incorporating many of the simpler principles into the hardware, programmers can concentrate on the real problems. For example, if you are trying to work with a robot arm the programming problem is much simplified if the arm itself can co-ordinate its movements using feedback implemented as hardware.

Intelligent or just clever?

There is a very thin dividing line between clever programming and artificial intelligence. Indeed, it is possible that there is no such thing as an intelligent program — just clever programs that become increasingly clever. For example, Chapter Seven described a very simple program that would carry on a limited conversation. The limitations of this program are mainly to do with the rather crude method that lay behind the program. By detecting the presence of certain keywords within sentences the Eliza program can offer relevant, if not meaningful, sentences in return. For example, if you were to use a sentence with the word 'why' in it, the program might give an answer along the lines of "Some questions are difficult to answer", a vague, enigmatic response which serves in most situations! If you want to try a small experiment just say "Some questions are difficult to answer" in response to anything said to you that contains the word 'Why'. To improve on the program also smile or frown depending on whether or not you judge the situation to be light hearted or serious'! Apart from being a little boring, you will find that this automatic response is accepted by a large number of people.

The point to be noted is that by applying some very simple rules you can give the impression of intelligence. Human beings are intelligent and, if you can raise their expectations to a high enough level, they will try to interpret almost anything as evidence of intelligence in someone or something else. In the case of computers, the public's expectations have been raised almost to the roof and it is fairly easy to convince an innocent onlooker that some trivial program or other is the cleverest thing in the universe.

Machines quickly become endowed not only with human intelligence but also with human personality and this is nothing new. In the days of steam engines huge hunks of brass and steel were often referred to as 'she' or even by a first name! Humans are very, very willing to lend some of their intelligence and personality to the simplest of machines. The computer dialogue program Eliza first saw the light of day very early on in the history of computers, let alone AI. Computers were so new at the time that a considerable number of people were taken in by its performance and had deep and meaningful conversations with it. So seriously was it taken that psychiatrists wanted to use it with real patients and, as mentioned in Chapter Seven, patients even preferred it! If you think that we have

Approaching intelligence

now reached the point of much greater sophistication that simple Eliza-like programs would be old hat and unimpressive, you would be disappointed. Eliza is still trotted out as an example of computer intelligence rather than as an historical event and the public (and many computer scientists) are still taken in!

This willingness to believe in the intelligence of computers has two important aspects. Firstly, as has been mentioned a number of times earlier, it means that we can achieve some useful results without too much effort by borrowing some of the user's intelligence. Secondly, it cautions us that we must ourselves beware of becoming believers too easily!

The Turing test

The traditional way of guarding against being taken in and believing that a clever program has achieved intelligence is the so called 'Turing test', named after Alan Turing who first proposed it. The basic idea is that any program that claims intelligence should be tested against a human, the only certain form of intelligence that we know of. This test consists of placing the program and the human in a box and allowing other humans to communicate with both over a VDU or some other common means of communication. If the external observers cannot tell with any certainty which is the computer program and which is the human then for all practical purposes the program may be called intelligent. This simple test has many problems, for example, should the human make an active effort to conceal or reveal the truth, but it is appealing as a description of what we should expect from an intelligent program. The main trouble is that the Turing test is a 'black box' test in that the observers do not worry themselves about how things are working inside the boxes, only that the outputs are appropriate. The reason why this is a problem is that it is possible that a program will pass the Turing test and receive the label 'intelligent' but to the computer scientists who created it seems rather more simple in its workings than true human intelligence. Some programs can already pass limited forms of the Turing test where the questions that the observers can put to the program are restricted to a narrow range of topics. For example, chess programs are now so good that it takes a master to tell the difference between a human player and a program. In this sense, a chess program is intelligent when the Turing test is restricted to questions about games of chess but, as we know, the program uses methods that are unlikely to be the exactly the same ones that humans use. A chess program searchs a move tree, uses exact evaluation functions, applies heuristic rules and remembers openings and endgames more accurately than any human ever could. In other words, much of its performance comes from clever programming combined with the raw speed of calculation offered by a computer. Another problem with the Turing test is that in some senses it is too easy to pass. For example, if you put the Eliza program in a box then the chances are that you could find someone who was convinced that it was intelligent. Does this give us the right to claim that Eliza is intelligent? Clearly not but in a sense it has passed the Turing test!

A suitable modification of the Turing test to take account of the special abilities of some programs and the varying abilities of humans would be to award a sort of IQ mark for that subject as the ratio of people who believe that the program is intelligent. For example, if computer chess can convince say 80% of the population that, as far as chess is concerned, it is intelligent then this is a rough measure of its IQ. To make this measurement more exact it would have to take into account the specific IQs of the people that it convinced it was intelligent, i.e.,

Specific IQ = average of the specific IQs of all the people who
of program   decide that the program passes the Turing test

The advantage of this definition is that it allows us to tell when a program has reached the level of the average human performing the task and removes the current emphasis on the computer 'beating the best'. It also changes the Turing test into a measure (the Turing measure?) of program intelligence rather than a once and for all pass/fail type test. Of course, all of this begs the question of how you measure the specific human IQs but this is a problem for psychology (or psychometrics to be precise).

Of course, human intelligence is different from any of the abilities measured by the specific IQs in that it is general, but what does this mean? In the case of the chess program it is easy to see that while it might score a high chess IQ, it would have IQs on other subjects so close to zero that it would make no difference! A human chess player, on the other hand, would obtain a non-zero score on a range of specific IQ tasks and this is the clearest indication that the general IQ of humans differs from the extremely specific IQs of programs. The long-term aim of AI is to produce a program that mimics enough of human behaviour to score something significantly larger than zero on an open-ended range of specific IQ tests.

Is intelligence computable?

The long-term goal of AI is in itself something that is cause for controversy. Some people follow the cybernetics argument that humans are just special cases of a more general principle that lies behind all machines, i.e. humans are not distinctly different from their creations. This viewpoint has a simplicity that makes it very attractive. It also has a long history without anyone being able to come up with conclusive evidence that it is wrong! Indeed as biology progresses more and more of the human and other animal systems are explained in the same mechanistic language that we use for our machine creations. Once it was thought that life contained some magical quality that inanimate objects lacked – a sort of life force that was different and not part of the rest of the physical world. Now we describe life in terms of chemical reactions that reduce even the human body to a mechanism sharing much in common with the simple steam machine! This is just another aspect of a general trend that tends to make the human system less and less different from the rest of the universe. Initially there was opposition to the view that humans shared characteristics with animals, let alone the inanimate world of machines. Then, with the acceptance of Darwinian evolution, the distinction between man and animals was weakened. As science progresses, the distiction between physical animal and physical machine also becomes less and less clear – more a difference in the technology used to implement the same principles. The attempt to remove the last distinction between humans and machines in AI's goal of producing intelligent computers can be seen as yet another stage in this progression. However, the steady progress of the mechanistic explanation is not a guarantee that there will ever be a successful reduction of the world to machine principles. Apart from postulating some magic quantity that humans have that creates intelligence, it is difficult to guess at the nature of what might keep us from producing intelligence in machines.

There is a general belief that given sufficient time and sophistication a computer-like machine could solve any problem. This is one of the false cornerstones of an often-heard argument that computers will one day be as intelligent as we are. The flaw in the argument is that we already know a lot of problems that are not computable! The exact arguments that are involved in showing that there exist problems that are not computable involve a lot of mathematics and the problems themselves are fairly esoteric and difficult to describe. Perhaps the simplest and most relevant is that it is impossible to write a program that can determine whether any given program will ever stop. In other words, it is impossible to write a program that will accept the code that defines a program and print out a message that will indicate whether it will stop or run for ever! This means that the 'stopping' problem is non-computable. The discovery that there are such non-computable problems came as something of a shock to the scientific community and there have been many attempts to make use of its relevance in the discussion of human intelligence. The real question is "do humans contain anything that cannot be programmed into a computer that makes it impossible for a computer to achieve intelligence?" In other words, "is intelligence computable?"

The steady progress in the reduction of all things, animal and human, to the machine is in one sense encouraging to the belief that intelligence is computable. However, this steady progression meets something of a discontinuity when it reaches intelligence. The important difference is that intelligence and computers are both products of the human brain and while the brain can understand the workings of the body and other machines the idea that it can understand itself is a little more startling! Indeed there is something akin to the program halting problem — ie., a program examining other programs — in a brain that examines itself and we know that the halting problem is non-computable!

I am not suggesting that intelligence is non-computable. Rather the status of intelligence is currently a matter of belief that the steady progress of AI will ultimately lead to an intelligent machine.

Is AI different?

There is a point of view that says that AI is not really different from normal programming and computer science. This is certainly true in that so far we have failed to write any programs that can claim to be intelligent. No AI program written to date uses anything so difficult that it would not be recognised and understood by a good programmer. The trouble is that it is difficult to see how you can write a program that you can claim is intelligent when you also know in great detail how it works! In this sense, AI is a subject chasing a moving target. Every time we manage to write a program that does some task that we thought required intelligence we know exactly how it works and so the task becomes demoted to the ranks of automation. An intelligent program would have to be such that it fooled not only its audience, like the Eliza program, but also fooled its creators and this is something it is difficult to imagine.

Even though as yet there is not the magic of real machine intelligence to mark AI out from other areas of programming, there is a collection of methods that it can call its own. The idea of an algorithm loosely applied as a heuristic is something that characterises AI programs. The tree structure seems to crop up so often in a wide range of apparently different problems that it deserves to be called the fundamental data structure of AI. Indeed you could say that the tree is to AI what the array is to mathematical programming. Much AI theory comes from other disciplines — logic, philosophy, probability etc — but these appear with lesser frequency. Even so, the AI programmer needs to be something of a polymath.

Where next?

For the first time AI is being taken seriously as a branch of computer science. To an extent the reason for this is a realisation that if the millions of personal computers already sold and the millions of more powerful machines yet to be designed are going to be used it has to be with the help of AI programs. There is no way that in the future the number of programmers can increase at the same rate as the number of computers and computer applications. There has always been a shortage of skilled manpower in computing and there seems to no prospect of this changing!

If computers are ever going to be a help to us they must cease to be the preserve of scientists, technologists and programmers and become universal assets that everyone can get something out of. It will always be true that some people will get more out of computers than others — it is likely that there will still be AI researchers in the future! — but the objective is to lower the threshold of knowledge necessary to begin using a computer. To this end it is important that part of the development of AI concentrates on producing flexible systems that can interact with humans to supply and record knowledge.

The computer as an intelligence amplifier is an attractive idea that we are still a long way from implementing. Today most of the mutual working together of man and machine is on the machine's terms! It is possible to see the steady development of software in terms of how much allowance it makes for its human user. The early 'first generation' software was concerned with getting the job done and paid little attention to the convenience of its users. 'Second generation' software tended (and tends) to approach the same range of applications in roughly the same way but in addition it attempts to be 'user-friendly'. The term 'user-friendly' is difficult to define but it can be interpreted to mean that the software will inform the user of any mistakes that he makes and give him another chance to get it right (an approach which should be contrasted to first generation software which would simply print an error message and give up!) 'Third generation' software is just beginning to appear and it is characterised by the assumption that any mistakes or misunderstandings are its own failing! For example, a first generation data base program would expect enquiries to be in a fixed format that was suited to its workings and any enquiry that did not conform to this format would simply be rejected. A second generation data base program would be slightly better in that it would use a fixed format more in keeping with the way the user wanted to make enquiries. It would detect any deviation from the fixed format and request that the user correct the enquiry. A third generation data base program would not force the user to enter enquiries in anything other than the most natural format and any failure to understand a sensible enquiry would be taken to be the program's fault! It would attempt to avoid repeating the fault by learning the meaning of the new type of enquiry from the user rather than forcing the user to learn another way of making the enquiry.

The ultimate goal of AI is to produce human-like intelligence in a non-human machine. Whether this can be achieved in a reasonable amount of time, or indeed ever, is not a question that alters the practical importances of producing programs that take us further along the road toward the goal. The new generation of programs that AI is producing should be the start of the gradual change from the machine's way of doing things to the flexible, intelligent way.

Further reading

The literature concerning AI divides into two categories: theoretical discussions of how things might be done and descriptions of how things have been done. Although the theoretical discussions are sometimes useful, without the constraint of the real world in the form of programming they tend to drift into the realms of philosophy! The best AI books tell you something practical that is based on theory!

There are a large number of introductory text books on AI. Among my favourites are:

Artificial Intelligence, by P H Winston, Addison Wesley, 1977
A down-to-earth description of a wide range of topics including an introduction to the main AI programming language, Lisp.

Artificial Intelligence and Natural Man, by M Boden, Harvester Press, 1977
A good non-technical introduction to AI.

There are a huge number of AI books on specific topics and so it is not possible to give a list of everything that is worth reading. Some that I have found useful are:

Build Your own Expert System, by C Naylor, Sigma Technical Press, 1983
This book uses Bayesian decision making as an introduction to expert systems. It is worth looking at for an alternative approach.

Expert Systems in the Micro Electronic Age, edited by D Michie, Edinburgh University Press, 1979
The best guide to practical expert systems and very readable once you have mastered the fundamentals.

Brains, Machines and Mathematics, by M A Arib, McGraw Hill, 1964
A good but slightly mathematical guide to cybernetics and the biological approach generally.

Computer Gamesmanship, by D Levy, Century Publishing Co, 1983

Index

Aardvark program, 43
Address, 68
Algorithm, 10
Associative memory, 69

BASIC, 8
Bayes' theorem, 53

Computability, 8, 118
Computer-aided intelligence, 3
Computer chat program, 105
Computer memory, 65
Conceptual data base program, 73
Conceptual store, 72
Conditional probability, 52
Cross correlation, 90
Cybernetics, 114

Eliza program, 110, 116
Evaluation function, 29
Expert system, 40

Feature, 85, 91
Feature space, 92
Fuzzy logic, 56

Heuristic, 9, 17, 27, 38
Human memory, 65

Intelligence, 4

Language, 100
Learning, 82
LISP, 8

Meaning, 109
Memory, 65
Microsoft BASIC, 8
Minimax, 34
Move tree, 21

Noughts and crosses program, 29, 57

Parsing, 103
Pattern recognition, 82
Perceptron, 96
Pragmatic syntax, 110
Probability, 51
Problem solving, 7, 9, 41
Production rule, 103
Prolog, 8

RAM, 7
Relational stores, 71

Semantics, 101, 108
Speech recognition, 6
Syntax, 101

Template matching, 86
Tile game program, 11, 24
Tree, move, 21
Turing test, 117
Two-person game, 28
Two-ply search, 23, 34

Vision, computer, 5